A Time of My Life - by the Grace of God

by

Norene Nygaard

authorHOUSE®

AuthorHouse™
1663 Liberty Drive, Suite 200
Bloomington, IN 47403
www.authorhouse.com
Phone: 1-800-839-8640

This book is a work of non-fiction. Unless otherwise noted, the author and the publisher make no explicit guarantees as to the accuracy of the information contained in this book and in some cases, names of people and places have been altered to protect their privacy.

First published by AuthorHouse 9/24/2007

ISBN: 978-1-4343-2106-0 (sc)

Printed in the United States of America
Bloomington, Indiana

This book is printed on acid-free paper.

Dedication

To my mother and dad, Hannah and Otto Nygaard, who
loved me enough to say "No" to my many whims. It was
even a part of my name. "No, NOrene" were two words I
frequently heard. Without those two words, I'm sure I would
have fallen off the limb even more often than I did.

To my brother and sister, Noran and Myrtice, who cared
enough to allow me to be my"free-spirited" self, who
encouraged me to tell seldom-told-tales, and who refrained,
sometimes with difficulty, from saying: "you can't say that"!

Most of all, to my Lord and Savior, Jesus Christ,
Who has been with me all the days of my life,
guiding me and forgiving me over, and over, and over!

Acknowledgments

I gratefully acknowledge my appreciation to my
friend and neighbor, Holly Westerberg, who
spent countless hours typing and editing.

And to my friends, Dorothy Hopps, Gaetano Benza, and
Chuck Rollason for their continued support during the
writing process, as well as to the many friends who have
told me for years that I had a story that must be told.

Table of Contents

The twins

Myrtice, Noran & Norene

Chapter 1
Growing Up On A Farm and Ranch

I was born in 1926 in Central Texas, between Meridian and Cranfills Gap, in a farmhouse on a farm and ranch. My mother, who weighed less than 100 pounds, had a double whammy – twins! We were named Noran and Norene. There were five sets of twins in our community.

My mother, Hannah, had been a school teacher for seven years before she married. As a wedding gift, my mother and dad each got the down payment from their parents to purchase two farms. In addition, they also received a wagon, two mules, and a grain reaper.

Mother had a horse and buggy that she had used when she taught school. However, some days she just rode her horse to school. I always wondered why she gave up teaching to marry and work like a slave on the farm.

She was very smart and loved teaching, but in those days, once a lady married, she gave up the teaching profession. However, there was so much work to be done on the farm, so there was no way a person could have done both. I always felt that she had made a bad choice in becoming a farmer's wife.

My dad, Otto Nygaard, had grown up on a farm, and when they married, he bought a 175 acre farm. He had to work very hard, not only to make payments on the farm, but to also buy plows, a tractor, horses, mules, seed, sheep, chickens, and cattle. He also had a smaller farm until the Great Depression hit on October 29, 1929. He sold the smaller farm because he was unable to make land bank payments on both farms.

This particular time in America was called the "Roaring 20's". Everyone all over America was making good money. They figured prosperity would be endless. Many of the families in our Norwegian community were paying to bring other family members over from Norway. Most of the families in the community had bought farms and raised cattle, sheep, goats, horses, hogs, and chickens as their livelihood.

Then suddenly, the "Great Depression" hit. I was only 3 years old at the time, but I remember in the years that followed how hard everyone worked to survive the hardships.

The drilling of an oil well was started near our community grocery store, which was about a mile from our farm. We were all excited, as this would have led to much more drilling in our area. Everyone met at a booth that served us homemade cookies and cold lemonade. All the children were given balloons, and we played together as our parents visited with their friends. However, as luck would have it, during the depression when we desperately needed help, the company ran out of money before they were able to strike oil.

My dad was very interested in politics. He especially worked hard to get his favorite county commissioner elected. Whoever was elected would determine whether or not my dad would have a job on construction and maintenance of county roads for the next two years. In 1932, this extra job was a matter of survival during the depression years. Daddy got the job and to acknowledge his appreciation, he dropped by the commissioner's house to thank him and at the same time, gave him a loaf of mother's bread.

I remember when the candidates would give their political speeches, there would be an "all you can eat" barbecue and soft drinks served to the many families who attended. One year the barbecue was held at Barney's Place, near Meridian, and another time out in the woods at a community farm.

One time we drove to Hamilton to see and hear W. Lee O'Daniel, who was running for governor that year. We especially enjoyed the day because his children, Pat, Mike, and Molly played and sang in his band, which was called "The Light Crust Doughboys". He previously had worked at the Burris Mills in Fort Worth. One of the main planks in his platform was to initiate the Old Age Pension, which our grandparents were subsequently beneficiaries of that program. That gave each of them about fifteen dollars a month, which was a big help during the depression years.

Once a year we had the opportunity to spend a delightful afternoon at the Hico Reunion. It was exciting for us to ride the merry-go-round and the ferris wheel. We ate cotton candy, carried a big balloon, and had our picture taken so we would have a souvenir of our enjoyable day.

One of the highlights of living on the farm, was during Christmas when Daddy would come out of the woods with a cedar tree that would soon become our "Christmas tree". We would sometimes walk along the creek or on the edge of the mountain months in advance, trying to figure out which was the prettiest tree to chop down for Christmas. My brother, sister, and I would then decorate the tree. We had real five-inch candles all over the tree. They were fitted into little holders which clipped onto the tree. The smell of cedar, along with the smell of apples and oranges under the tree is something I still remember.

We were always happy with the toys we received on Christmas morning. We received cars, trucks, and dolls to play with in our little sandpile in front of the house. I also enjoyed coloring books and crayons which kept us busy on cold or rainy days. One year, we got a red wagon, and we pushed and pulled each other around in it. We also learned that each of us could put a knee in the wagon, and push off with our other foot. With the handle pulled back to hold onto, away we went down the hills!

We always got something new to wear as one of our gifts under the tree. One year, Noran and I both received a matching blue sweater, scarf, mittens, and hat to match. This kept us warm as we walked to and from school in the second and third grades. I can still remember what it was like to come home from school on a cold day and Mother would have a big pot of beans and hot rolls waiting, or else a big pot of soup with a big bone on the side to pick off some meat.

We didn't get anywhere near the amount of gifts that kids receive these days. But we were always excited about Christmas and thankful for all our gifts. I remember painting my toy car black with Daddy's paint so I could identify my car from Noran's car. The red wagon was later used to aid in doing our errands, such as bringing in wood or filling it full of corn to haul to the pig pen.

I had a sister, Myrtice, who was five years older. We often "played school" and she was always the teacher. She knew as a child that one day she would become a teacher. She had so much determination in everything she attempted to do, that it was clear to many that she was a "born leader".

Noran and I were born October 22, so because of our age, in September we couldn't qualify to start school until mid-term. Because my mother and sister taught us at home, Noran and I went to school only a few months in the first grade. I remember that someone came to school to vaccinate us. I had on long sleeves, so they pulled my dress off. I was terrified as everyone watched "the show". Someone stood in front of me, but they weren't big enough to hide me! I think I cried partly because of my pain and partly because of my humiliation. That's about all I remember of the first grade.

In the second grade, I heard my teacher telling my dad at a PTA meeting how smart Noran was. He asked, "How's Norene doing?" She said that she's okay, but Noran is the genius! That didn't help my confidence, so when I took the next test, I scooted over to one side of my seat to give Jesus room to sit and to help me. Jesus helped me pass, but I decided He must not be the genius Noran was, because my report card didn't reflect a straight A+ grade--like Noran's card!

Years later, I discovered that part of my problem was my teacher.

She taught me for the first three years of school. I was left-handed, and she would jerk the pencil out of my left hand and put it in my right hand. When she wasn't looking, it would go back to my left hand so I could complete my work on time. She would catch me, and make me do it right-handed. She told my parents that they should make me eat right-handed and continue with her work while I was at home. I couldn't possibly finish every lesson on time, so my report card would show A's and B's instead of A+'s like my brother's card.

It wasn't fair! I knew the answers, but didn't have time to finish the assignment. My dad would not sign my report card for about a week, so the teacher would have plenty of time to humiliate me in front of the class, by letting everyone know why my report card didn't get signed. It wasn't like I was the "dummy" of the class, I was probably in the top five as I went through school.

Years later, when I was in college, I did a research paper on handedness, and was informed from all the books that I researched, that a child should never be forced to change hands. For one thing, it would likely make a nervous wreck out of the child. My education teacher pointed out after I made the report, that I came through it quite well in spite of my teacher.

He pointed out by saying, "How many of your classmates would have made the grades you did, had they been forced to write with their left hand?"

But the research helped me to forgive my teacher, when I found out that when she got her education, teachers were told to have the children make the change. I also found information that one side of the brain rules the intellectual side of us, and the other side rules the creative side. By nature, I was very creative. God just had me wired up to think differently than my siblings and friends.

One more thing I remember about the second grade, was that one of my classmates came to school and told the teacher that the reason she had been absent was that her mother had a baby, and it became an angel and went to heaven. We dared not lie at my house, and I wondered if she was telling the truth. I went up to the teacher's desk and whispered, "Do you think a baby can sprout wings and go to heaven?"

The teacher told me that she had not talked to her mother, so she wasn't sure what had happened. (Of course, the baby had died, but death hadn't been explained to me like that.) For many years, after that day, I would dream that I could flap my arms up and down and run, and then suddenly I could fly! Not that I wanted to be an angel, but flying seemed like an exciting thing to do. I would fly towards Cranfills Gap, but would awaken before I arrived there. The flying made me feel wonderful and free. It seemed strange that I should dream this so often, but it was always a happy feeling to get away from my normal existence! Years later, while I was in college, I checked out a library book on dreams, and found that dreaming of flying was a sign of needing to get out more and mix with more people.

I also experienced many dreams of dancing around a castle. If there is anything to reincarnation, I could write a book on those constant dreams. You will find out more about my dancing a little later. Dancing was as natural to me as breathing!

My wild imagination gave me many experiences. Before I started school, I had imaginary friends, and they had names. My best friend's name was Cackeltootie, who had three children, Smirie, Murrie, and Musmurrie. When I started to school, my aunt told me that I would have many friends to play with, and should start forgetting my imaginary ones. I had to tell them "good-bye". It was a hard thing to do. However, I loved animals, and they became my best friends.

In the summertime, it was too hot to sleep inside the house, so I would pile a bunch of quilts on the front porch. All the cats and dogs would come and sleep with me. I named all the animals – even the cows and pigs had names. I guess that was a pretty good sign that I needed more play time to be with other children.

Fortunately, I became interested in reading books, but had trouble understanding the difference between fact and fiction. I'd go ask my mom if the story was real or make-believe (fantasy). I can now see why my dreams, my imaginary friends, and stories all seemed so real to me. I figured that "Cinderella" was real, and I thought that surely "Titanic" was fiction. I had found Mother's book upstairs, and read it at an early age. I couldn't believe all those people had drowned in the cold ocean.

My mother and sister had all kinds of books around the house. I would memorize nursery rhymes from Myrtice's books. I liked reading because it gave me a rest from the frustration of having to use my right hand. I was made to feel like an odd-ball because I wrote, ate, and thought a little differently than everyone else.

I figured no one really understood how I felt, except maybe my dog, Queen. I guess that is why I have had dogs all my life. They give so much love and understanding and are never judgmental. I believe the best day I remember on the farm is when Daddy came home from Meridian with this beautiful collie, named Queen.

Noran and I each managed to get the measles, chicken pox, and mumps at the same time! We would sit in bed and play checkers, dominoes, and a card game called "Old Maid" and another one called "Go Fishing". There was a large picture above the head of the bed that had "Home Sweet Home" written on it. There was a tune by that same name that Daddy would play on the accordion.

One day, Noran picked up Daddy's old accordion and played it. Then he showed me how to play. We knew how to play the harmonica, so it was easy. (When you blow out on the harmonica, you push together on the accordion, and when you draw your breath in on the harmonica is when you pull out on the accordion) We surprised Daddy that afternoon when he came home from the field. We played the song, "Home Sweet Home". He was proud of us and every time someone would come for a visit, he would ask us to play and sing for them. We all liked to sing and play the accordion. Music has a way of making most people happy, so it was good therapy for hard workers.

Of course, everyone from Texas loved Bob Wills. We had heard him for years yelling, "Take it away, Leon!" We learned to sing all of his songs, as well as those of Eddy Arnold, Hank Williams, Ernest Tubb, Gene Autrey, and many more. There was a riddle of the time: "Do you know why Bob Wills never got drunk?" Answer: "Because Leon kept taking it away."

Anytime there was a Gene Autrey or Roy Rogers show in Meridian, Noran and I would go see it twice while our parents talked to all their friends on the street corners and did the grocery shopping for the following week.

As hard as we worked, we did get to take off to see movies that were important to us. We also saw all the Will Rogers movies.

I grew up with a couple of "free-spirited" relatives –- Uncle Emil Olson and his first cousin, Eddie Paulson. They spent part of their time being "railroad bums". They would jump on a freight train to get a free ride across the country to see new sights and meet new people. When they would run out of money, they would do different jobs for a little food and a little cash. They could work in fields, break wild horses, and do many odd jobs.

When they weren't traveling, they would often stay with us and help Daddy with some field work so they could make a few bucks. They would sleep upstairs, and were very much a part of our family. Uncle Emil was a great story teller. He would tell us of their experiences. Eddie liked to sing and play the harmonica. He taught us how to sing, how to play the harmonica, and how to yodel. There was a favorite song he would often sing, and we would all sing along with him.

> "All around the water tank, waiting for a train;
> A thousand miles away from home, sleeping in the rain.
> I haven't got a nickel, not a penny can I show
> Get off, get off, you railroad bum
> And he slammed the boxcar door.
> Yodel "Eddie", Yodel "Eddie", Yodel "Eddie".

(Eddie was the one who taught us, so we sang it as Yodel Eddie)

Sometimes, we would go out on the front porch and sing songs, and play harmonicas. Daddy would play the accordion. Mother would make some ice cream, and Myrtice would crank the handle until it was frozen and ready to eat.

A few years back, Noran and I were in a record shop at the Fort Worth Stock Yards and heard the song being sung by Box Car Willie. Of course, he bought the record in memory of our second cousin, Eddie, and our Uncle Emil and all the experiences they shared with us.

Every day, all year long, we had our daily duties of feeding the animals, milking the cows, gathering the eggs, and bringing in the wood for the cook stove. In winter months, we also brought in wood for the pot-belly heater in the living room. We were taught that sometimes we had to do things that maybe we didn't want to because it would build our character! It was also a matter of survival.

I have been told that instead of whining about how hard I had to work, I should be thankful that we had plenty of food to eat, and that we were so safe that we never thought of locking a door, even when we went somewhere. Well, I am thankful that I had the energy to help plant, cook, and can the food that we had.

That being said, before we call the kettle black, have I mentioned that we worked in 100 degree weather, and when we got back to the house, there were no fans to cool us? We studied by coal oil lamps, for there was no electricity in the country homes. We carried in our drinking water and heated it on the stove for dishwashing and baths. We had an out-house, and the Sears and Roebuck and Montgomery Ward catalogues were recycled out there.

Ever so often, some strangers would come on the farm and tie ribbons onto bushes and posts. I kept hoping they would bring equipment out to drill an oil well, but to add to my disappointment, it never happened.

We did have a telephone on the wall, and a certain ring was designated for each family. Ours was one short and three long rings. In other words, whoever was lonesome or "nosey" could listen to other peoples phone calls.

I remember during the war, a friend called me from California, and before I hung up the phone, I heard a half dozen "clicks". When I got on the school bus the next morning, everyone knew when my date would be back in Texas.

Back to our survival during the depression years - the only way I know how to explain how we came through it all, is that we prayed before each meal.

By thanking God, He always provided for us. We were brought up with the fear, as well as the love of God. At night, we prayed that if we should die before we wake, we pray the Lord our soul to take. We knew we had to make everything right with our siblings and friends, if we had shown any anger that day. I wonder who wrote these prayers for kids. Thinking about dying before the next day can scare the hell out of a kid!

I am thankful, however, that we were taught that God would never give us more than we can handle. That has kept me from crumbling through years of adversity. I am grateful that God did provide for us at all times. Through all our praying, I don't remember ever going hungry. Faith in God makes you tough, and you can take anything. There is a saying, "Tough times never last, but tough people do."

We learned never to waste our time or money. We had wild plums and grapes growing along the field fences, and we would make jelly and jam.

We used our time to plant enough vegetables to eat. Then we would can the rest for the winter months. We had plenty of chickens and hogs to provide us with protein. We were not to waste anything. We were supposed to eat everything on our plates, because there were people in other countries starving. I ate everything, and they are still starving!

However, each child did give a few nickels and pennies in Sunday School class that was sent to the poor people overseas. At the church service we gave more for the missions. But by giving, we truly learned that we also received. Otherwise, I really could not explain how we survived the depression. A stick of gum would last a week. At night, I'd stick it on the bed post. I had another "cud" stuck under my desk at school.

I have to admit, I always resented that we were so poor. Any money we made would go for additional animals or farm implements. Then there was the land bank note to be paid. I wanted a new house, or at least some paint put on the one we had! I had a burning desire to burn down the house, but I had sense enough to know that instead of getting a new house, we would probably end up living in one of the three barns on the farm.

IF WORK DOESN'T KILL YOU, IT WILL MAKE YOU STRONG. I could relate to the black people because I had been told about slavery. The jobs that Myrtice, Noran, and I did on the farm just during the summertime would make slaves feel as though they were born free! For two weeks during the summer, we would go to Vacation Bible School for half a day. We walked two miles every morning and two miles back in the heat of the day. There was work to be done when we got home!

We had a peach orchard with two dozen peach trees. You can imagine how many peaches there were to pick, peel and can! When that job was completed, we would go to the fields to gather a load of corn. We would shuck, cut, cook, and can a hundred cans a day! There were also beans, tomatoes, squash, peas and other seasonal vegetables to be picked and canned. We would spend hours digging up potatoes, onions, carrots, and beets. Anything that had been planted in the garden was never to be left there. After we got all we needed, we filled boxes for the preacher, relatives, or anyone who didn't have a garden.

But that didn't end the summer! We also picked cotton, shocked grain, brought in corn for the pigs and chickens, and grain for the cattle, so the animals would have plenty to eat during the winter. We ground up wheat to add to the flour my mother needed to make fresh home-made bread about four times a week. She could make the best home-made bread of anyone in the community. There was nothing like the smell of hot rolls as we walked into the house at noon.

Myrtice was "Daddy's Big Helper". He always said that Myrtice could do anything, and she really could. She was healthy and strong as a brick wall, and could keep up with any man in the fields. She could pick a hundred pounds of cotton to my thirty pounds. I simply hated the fields! In the back of my head I kept the thought that some day, some way, I'd get off the farm. I would think that maybe I could learn to sing or dance, or in my wildest imagination, become a movie star. Every time my dad would brag about what a hard worker she was I felt like saying, "Frankly, my dad, I don't give a damn!" (I had just seen the movie, "Gone With the Wind", and we all giggled and laughed when Clark Gable said that word.)

Myrtice was also "Mama's Little Girl". They made quilts, clothing, embroidered cup towels, and made cotton-picking sacks. They also enjoyed planting a garden, cooking, and canning. I did what I had to as a matter of survival, but my heart wasn't into farming. (Did I mention we were paid about seventy-five cents for every hundred pounds of cotton we picked? It took two to three days for me to earn a dollar!)

Noran probably worked harder on the farm than any slave was ever expected to. When he was 8-10 years old, he milked cows, worked in the fields, and drove the tractor. I don't ever remember hearing him complain. My job was to gather the eggs, feed the chickens, and carry in wood for the cook stove. Later, I milked one gentle cow. I didn't mind that, as she was one of my best friends.

I remember one summer, Noran decided to sleep during the heat of the day, and plow in the late evening into the night until it got so dark he couldn't see. Late one afternoon, I brought him some cold chocolate milk shake and sugar cookies. I told him I would drive the tractor and plow while he ate, drank, and relaxed. As I approached the first corner, I made a 45 degree turn instead of turning gradually. I glanced to the side and saw Noran running toward me and waving his arms to get my attention. The plow had raised up and almost flipped over because of my sharp turn. So that was the end of my plowing days!

When we were in high school, Noran drove one of the school buses. I remember a few days when he asked a neighbor to finish his route, so he could get off the bus, walk over the mountain, and start plowing in the field instead of going home first. That saved him time so he could finish plowing before it got too dark.

We had many rattlesnakes on the farm. When we shocked grain, we would often encounter a rattlesnake. Using rocks or hoes, we managed to kill some of them. Noran and I always carried pocket knives, so if one of us were to get snake bitten, the other one would cut the skin and suck the blood. We learned this from Noran's Boy Scout Book.

There were mountains on each side of the farm, and there were snake dens in each side of the mountains, where the Indians had lived. The snakes would hibernate in the dens all winter, and slither down into our fields in the spring and summer months. One of our neighbor girls lost her leg just below the knee because of a rattle snake bite. I hated them!

There were also chicken snakes but they were not so dangerous. Once, Noran and I were stacking hay in the barn above the chicken house. Daddy was pitching it up to us from the wagon, and we were putting the bundles in a neat pile at the back of the barn, so the animals would have plenty of feed during the winter months. All of a sudden, Noran plunged toward me. He saw a snake crawling up my pant leg! That was the end of my stacking hay for the day!

Once, I carried an arm full of wood into the house, and a little snake was hiding in the hollow of the log. When I threw the wood into the wood box, I saw the snake, and we had to open the doors and get brooms to chase it out of the house.

My cousin, Jesse Joel Olson, loved catching rattlesnakes. He had built a prong at the end of a broom handle, which he used to catch them. He'd put them in a cage and sell them to a pharmaceutical business that wanted rattlesnake venom. The skins were used to make western belts and boots.

We had another relative who was bitten by a rattlesnake. He grabbed it, wrung it's head, threw it down and then drove himself to the hospital 15 miles away!

MY THOUGHTS WERE THAT IF WORK DIDN'T KILL YOU, THE RATTLESNAKES WOULD GIVE IT A TRY!

One day, Myrtice, Noran, and I went out to the field to gather a load of corn. When we filled the wagon, I was hot and tired, so I jumped up on the wagon and decided to ride on the corn instead of walking home. Noran drove the tractor, and Myrtice walked. By the time we got home, I was covered with scorpions.

They were in my hair and my clothing! I experienced terrible pain of scorpion stings. The only good thing about it was that I didn't have to help unload the wagon of corn!

One reason we had so much work to do was that times were hard, and Daddy would often take a job building roads in our county, as he knew how to handle the big equipment better than most men. Sometimes, he would go to West Texas to work in the harvest fields to make extra money.

I often thought I'd like to shake the hand of any slave who would prove he worked harder than we did. Daddy often told us that hard work never killed anyone. Maybe he was right. He certainly worked hard yet he lived to be 93 years old.

In spite of all the hard work, there was always time for some fun. I remember one time when the men in the community decided to present the PTA program with a woman-less wedding. You guessed it! A fat man was the bride, and a skinny man was the groom. My dad was one of the bridesmaids. The music began, "Here comes the bride, big, fat, and wide, and here comes the groom, as skinny as a broom." This brought the house down!

Another time, there was a minstrel show. The older people had grown up during the Broadway Days of the Ziegfield Follies, Fanny Brice, Al Jolson, and other popular stars of that era. One lady in the PTA played the piano. Daddy played the accordion. Someone painted Noran's face black with black shoe polish, and he did a tap dance which we called a jig. A black face was not meant to demean anyone, but it was during those early Broadway days when the black people got recognition for their rhythm. They could dance and play an instrument at the same time. Minstrels became popular in the 20's and reached us in the 30's with all the jazz and ragtime music.

Noran was only eight or nine years old when he was dressed up with a painted face and patches on his pants. Years later, I saw a little black boy at the Sky View Club in Fort Worth. He was smart enough to have a coffee can in front of him so those who watched him could throw in a few coins. I thought, "Now why didn't Noran think of doing that when we were so dirt poor?" (Now-a -days, it's called economically depressed.)

I learned to do the Charleston during that time, but I was no Fanny Brice! However, years later, I danced the Charleston in the lobby of a Dallas Theater in the 50's when the movie, "Has Anybody Seen My Gal?" came to the city. Also, to promote the show, I was asked to perform several different dances on the Jerri Johnson Variety Show on TV. Those were the fun days!

The first time I was ever out of Bosque County was in 1936, when we drove to Dallas to go to the Texas Centennial, which was at Fair Park. We stayed with Daddy's sister, Katie, and her family. Being in the city was like being in another country. We had a great time and came home with a shoe box full of souvenirs. I wore a pickle pin on my coat for the rest of the season. Noran and I were in the fourth grade at the time.

I had a new teacher and his name was Mr. Whitney. He started the days telling us what Amos and Andy said on the radio that morning. They were black and he could talk just like them. We had a radio, but we were not listening because we were milking cows and walking to school early each morning. Sometimes, Mr. Whitney and his wife would give us a party after school, and make us a big pot of soup or chili. We played learning games, like choosing sides and letting two at a time go up to the board and see who could be the first to find a certain country, state, or city on the map. Sometimes it would be a math problem.

I remember a snowy day when he let us go outside and have a snowball fight. On dry, cold days, we would often play "pop-the-whip". Then he would let us come in and stand around the big round stove to get warm, so we wouldn't get sick. There were many books in the room that we could read, and I don't believe he was ever upset with me. By now, I had learned to eat and write with my right hand. If he ever noticed me throwing a ball with my left hand, he never mentioned it to me. So I was happy to know that he would also teach me through the fifth grade. Our first five grades were spent in the Mustang community where we lived, near Cranfills Gap.

We started the sixth grade in Cranfills Gap, as the Mustang School had consolidated with the Cranfills Gap School. We no longer had to walk to school. A big, yellow, school bus picked us up at the gate to our farm. Wow! What did I ever do to deserve such luxury?

Norene

Cranfills Gap High School

Brady Cowan
-my first love

Noran

Myrtice

Noran plowing the fields in West Texas.

Chapter 2

Making It Through High School

I loved our new school at Cranfills Gap. It was the same town where we went to church, so we already knew many of our classmates. I had always claimed certain boys for my boy friends, but it never amounted to more than writing notes, or maybe carving their initials on a tree. But I remember one day when a class group ran by outside our room. One of the guys stopped, looked in the window, then waved. Everyone laughed! I asked those around me who the good looking guy was and they told me it was Brady Cowan.

His brother, Bonley, was one of my classmates, and we started calling one another "Bud" and "Sis". However, I was just in the sixth grade and knew that it would be a long time before I would begin dating.

When I got to High School, I still liked Brady, and wanted to date him. Daddy had it in his head that I couldn't date until I was sixteen years old.

I was getting many phone calls at fifteen, and by then, all my friends were dating. Most of my friends were a year older than I and it bothered me that I couldn't go out with them. One evening, when I got a phone call, I had to tell my friends that I couldn't go anywhere. My dad said, "Why are you pouting? You know the rules around here!"

I said, "Because all my friends get to have fun and all I can do is go to school, go to church, and go to the fields, and I am getting damn sick and tired of it!" Wow! I couldn't believe I said all that, and neither could my dad.

He got right up in my face and said, "I don't ever want to hear you talk like that again!" And he never did. I am not saying I never did; I'm just saying that he never heard me. From that day on, I knew that somehow, some way, someday, I was going to "get the hell off the farm"! I would get my own job, so I could have my own apartment, do as I please, feel free, and never, ever, let anyone be in control of my life again! But that was in the future. I was still too young and could not leave my parents.

As luck would have it, there came an opening for a cook with the thresher that summer. I needed a job, and I liked the challenge. There were always two cooks, and I wanted the job so badly, so I could make my own money. My dad happened to be in charge of the crew, so it took a little begging and cooking a few meals to prove to him that I could handle it. I was no gourmet cook, but how hard can it be to pour a little water over some vegetables, pitch in some salt to bring out the flavor and then boil it? I got the job! We cooked for about twenty-five people, five times a day. There was breakfast which was bacon, eggs, toast, and coffee. There was a mid-morning snack, lunch, mid-afternoon snack, then supper. I can still remember the first night slicing bacon until 11:00 o'clock to get ready for the next day's work. Everyone slept on cots. One guy who always slept with his glasses on, was to get up early and warm up the engines. He would blow the whistle, which was the wake -up call. Young guys would play tricks on each other. The first night they put black soot on his glasses so the sun wouldn't wake him up.

On the second day, I fried some chicken while my partner made cookies and tea which she served to the crew for their mid-morning snack. Just as we got lunch ready, Dad came by and said that everything would be moved to the next farm before lunch. I put the chicken in the warming unit over the stove. By the time we arrived to the next farm, we had hit a few bumps on the country road. When we opened the cook shack door, all I could see was chicken all over the floor. I hurriedly picked it up and put it on the serving table. I was glad to see the men enjoying it, as I was in no mood to start over!

The cook shack must have been around 110 degrees, as we had no air conditioning in those days–not even a fan! After hanging my head outside the cook shack and throwing up for a while, the other cook spread a quilt under the cook shack and had me lie there until Noran came from the field with his load. He took me to the doctor at Cranfills Gap. The doctor said I had a heat stroke and sent me home with some salt tablets.

I was still very weak when the thresher came to our house, but I got out of bed and went out on the front porch and waved at everyone as they went by with their horses and wagons. Then came Daddy and the other boss with the engine and separator. I always called that my first job, even though it didn't last long. I did get paid for the two days that I worked.

After that, all I could think of was someday to have my own job, buy beautiful clothes, have my own money, and be independent and feel free. My hopeful mind began to see a rainbow after a storm. Of course, I had no earthly idea of the direction my life would take me. I was motivated by the early days of Broadway. It looked intriguing and would have beat the heck out of working in the fields for a living. However, I didn't have the talent or knowledge at that time to pursue such a career. So I just waited until I was older to make a move toward entertaining the public.

When I was about thirteen years old, I was chosen to be the narrator for the Christmas pageant at the church. I was so honored and thrilled to have the lead role in the program. I was an angel and recited the biblical Christmas story while baby Jesus was surrounded by Mary, Joseph, the shepherds, sheep, the three wise men, and singing angels. On the night of the play, in my excitement while rushing to get ready for the program, I stumbled and fell into the bath tub. I had just poured a kettle of boiling water into the tub, and before I could pour in the cold water, I slipped on a wet spot on the floor and fell forward into the boiling water. The burns immediately raised painful blisters on my hands. Mother anointed my hands with ointment, and gently wrapped them in gauze. I was in such pain, but wouldn't have thought of missing the program. Noran and the other wise men sang, "We Three Kings". I knew my part by memory, but I held the Bible in my hands, so the audience wouldn't notice my bandaged hands.

I often wondered what the future held for me. There were times when I thought that perhaps a singing career would be nice. I knew every song that came out in the "Hit Parade", which was a monthly song book with the words of the best hits. Noran and I were always asked to entertain for the PTA programs, and the Junior Luther League programs. We'd sing and play the accordion. We also belonged to the Cranfills Gap High School Band. Noran played the clarinet and I played the saxophone. This gave us a chance to put more variety into the programs. We could play the instruments by ear, so instead of playing the boring band tunes, we could come out with some popular tunes for the programs.

My friend, Delores Patterson, lived with her aunt and uncle, Bonnie and Jesse Windham. They had their own little musical group called the Windam Band. They would sometimes play at "honky tonks" on weekends. I spent a week-end with Delores and sang a few songs with the band. Noran walked in as I was singing, "I Only Want a Buddy, Not a Sweetheart". The place didn't have a good reputation. Neither of us were supposed to be there. Sometimes a guy was known to get into a fight outside during intermission, usually concerning some misunderstanding over someone dancing with his girlfriend.

The next time we went with them to Waco where no one knew us. You know how gossipy people are in small towns. They know everything you do, and by the time it is repeated several times, they make it sound like you are going to hell!

I enjoyed spending the weekend with Delores so we could enjoy an evening with the Windham Band. I thought it was fun to get up and sing at the clubs. This goes to prove that anyone with the guts to try something, can use their unlimited talent to accomplish anything they want to.

Music had such a huge effect on me. All I wanted to do was dance! Noran and I could really jitterbug together. He could flip me in the air, and like a cat, I'd land on my feet every time! People would clear the floor when we danced. Our favorite place to go dancing was at the Meridian State Park and Wildlife, always referred to as the Meridian Lake. It is a beautiful state park. The park had an open pavillion run by a one-armed tough guy, Tobe, who didn't take any nonsense from anyone. Everyone knew they must follow his rules. Being a state park, it was an ideal place for young school kids to enjoy, under the supervision of Tobe Gardner.

When we started going there, we were not yet sixteen, so we had to slip over there. We worked out a plan. Our parents let us go to the Junior Luther League on Sunday nights. We'd sing, play the accordion, and have a short prayer session. But when the group went outside to play ring games, we'd slip out to the car and take off for the Meridian Lake. A few of our friends either went with us, or met us there. What a great time we all had jitterbugging to "Boogie Woogie" and all the other popular tunes of the time.

Those were the World War ll years when we had gasoline rationing. Noran learned that he could use just a little gasoline to start the tractor, then switch to kerosene. In those days, gasoline cost ten cents a gallon and kerosene was about three cents a gallon. So that gave us that extra gallon we needed to get to the lake on Sunday nights! Of course, Daddy finally caught us sneaking off to the lake. But by now, we were almost sixteen and were allowed to "spread our wings" a little more.

We were involved in all the high school sports: volleyball, tennis, basketball, baseball. Noran also played football. I was a cheerleader, the drum major of the school band, and also sang in the school choir. Noran and I both sang in the church choir, while Daddy sang in the male chorus.

By now, Myrtice had managed to leave the farm, go to college, and was now teaching school. She was my parent's pride and joy. She made her own quilts, clothing, and could outwork any farm hand anyone would have. Now she was following in our mom's footsteps into the teaching profession.

Noran was very important, because he was the only male to carry on the Nygaard name. He was also a "walking encyclopedia". He could just glance at a book and make top grades in the class.

Then, there I was. Being gifted at creative things like singing or dancing didn't count. People thought that all I wanted to do was have a good time, and I guess they weren't too far off base. But at least, I was beginning to see the humorous side of life. I was always getting into trouble in school for giggling in class and passing notes to friends. My motto was, "Let the good times roll!"

One day, I told my friends to meet me on the stage during lunch hour and I would teach them to jitterbug. So instead of going outside after we had eaten, we went to the auditorium, pulled the curtains so that no one could see us, and I started teaching everyone how to jitterbug. About the second or third day, we got caught. The principal, Mr. Kruse, came up to the stage to tell everyone that they were supposed to be outside. We took off running, and some of us ran into the girls restroom. I yelled out, "I'll bet he won't come in here to find me!"

About that time, I heard the door open and a strong male voice say, "Norene, I want to talk to you." I went out and Mr. Kruse asked me what I was doing. I told him that I was just teaching everyone how to dance.

He asked, "Why were you doing that?"

I said, "Because they don't know how." He let me know this was not a dance school. So I got word to everyone that future instruction would be given at the Meridian Lake on Sunday nights!

I wasn't mean, so the teachers didn't punish me. I just didn't see why we couldn't laugh and have a good time while we were in school.

I thought we could just make the most of a restricted situation. I did read many books in my spare time. MARK TWAIN SAID, "HE WHO DOES NOT READ IS NO BETTER OFF THAN HE WHO CANNOT READ". I wrote a few book reports for friends who were too busy playing football to sit down and read the required number of books to complete our English courses. After all, what are friends for?

One thing I didn't like to read was history books, because there were too many dates to remember. I just couldn't see the value of knowing about the past. As a result, my teacher saw me at the back of the room giggling with a group of friends.

He said, "Norene, aren't you interested in learning what's in your history book?"

I said, "No, I am not interested in the past. I'm only interested in the present and the future." With that, he sent me across the hall to sit in the room with the principal, who was teaching a typing class. He came over to me and asked if I wanted to speak with him. I told him that my history teacher just told me to sit there while he taught history to the rest of the class. Just then, my two football friends walked in and sat down with me. They said that the teacher had remarked that if anyone was not any more interested than Norene to learn history, they could get up and join her across the hall. We just giggled a little more, and when the bell rang, we got out of there before the principal had a chance to ask any more questions. At least, we were being honest and were happy in our school. Teachers in this century would love to have that kind of problem these days, instead of weird kids on drugs or carrying guns.

There's an expression, "Sometimes we laugh to keep from crying." I was learning to rise above my problems. My biggest problem in school was giggling, passing notes, and having a good time. I wasn't ever mean to anyone. I liked everyone! I showed respect to my teachers, and they were nice to me, also.

One day in the study hall, one of the guys dared me to take a chew of tobacco. Well, I dared to try it, and I chewed it until it started coming out the side of my mouth. I raised my hand (which is what we did if we needed to go to the rest room). The little old lady teacher shook her head "no", so I spit it in the ink well on the desk, while we all had a big laugh. (People have asked, "What made you do so many crazy things?" I imagine God in heaven is still trying to figure that one out!)

The next day, instead of being in the study hall, I was assigned to go to Mr. Kruse's office. He didn't put me down, or even act like he knew what had happened.

He just said, "Norene, you are pretty good in bookkeeping class. I was wondering if you could come in every day for a while as my secretary and help me catch up on posting the absentee and tardy students." My friends knew why I was there, but I jokingly told them that I was Mr. Kruse's private secretary. After a few days, he thanked me for helping him get caught up.

That afternoon, the boys had a baseball game with the Gatesville Reformatory boys. My friend, Bill, threw the ball from the pitcher's mound to the first baseman, who missed it. I got hit on the jaw and saw stars! The principal, and my friend, Barber, carried me to the school house on a chair. They had me lie down on the couch in the principal's office. After the game, Bill came in and apologized for hitting me with the baseball.

I said. "You mean you were the one who threw the ball?" We started laughing.

I said, "Bill, you are always getting me into trouble! Here I am in the principal's office again!" That night, I had to play in the band.

While I played the saxophone, my jaw hurt so badly that tears rolled down my cheeks. But, the show must go on!

I was accustomed to bruises. Noran and I were always riding the little bulls on the farm and they would throw us off. We also rode bareback on the horses. We had a bridle but we didn't have a saddle, and we took a few tumbles during the early years of riding. We had a rodeo in Cranfills Gap every year, so we would imagine some day riding in the rodeo. Of course, that never happened.

During each of the last two years of high school we were allowed to have a class party. Bill and Barber asked if we could have it on the twins birthday, which was October 22nd. Both times the teacher let the class vote, and they all agreed. We enjoyed the attention we were given.

There were also disadvantages of becoming popular. For two straight years, the class voted me queen for the Halloween Carnival. I begged them not to vote for me because I didn't have an evening dress. I cried, and both years, Miss Hoff, my home economics teacher came through for me by borrowing a dress from one of the ladies in town. I liked Miss Hoff because she was a person who, somehow understood me. She had also been one of Mother's pupils. She was also my music teacher. She sang at weddings and funerals in the area, and I always told her how much I liked her singing.

There were a couple of weeks when she taught knitting and crocheting to our home economics class. Of course, I couldn't do it right handed, and she couldn't do it left handed. We even tried having me look in the mirror at her doing it, but we both gave up. She asked me if I would like to read during that time instead of knitting. Those were magic words for me. I read her books on how to entertain, how to plan a meal, how to set a table, etc. I always felt I was her favorite pupil after that. She was certainly my favorite teacher.

I was finally nearing my sixteenth birthday, and didn't have to sneak around anymore. All the school games and activities gave us a certain amount of freedom to get out and go. When I became sixteen, I let the world know that I would never, ever, be in anyone's control again! Best of all, I was no longer angry at my parents, but I would now live my life (hopefully) with few regrets. As Frank Sinatra sang, many years later, "I DID IT MY WAY!"

We were growing up now and no longer were we treated like little children. Now we were teenagers! Noran especially enjoyed playing football, while I was a cheerleader. When the band marched, I was the drum major. World War ll had taken our bus drivers, so a few of our most dependable younger boys were given a job of driving a school bus. Noran was asked to be one of those selected, so he was making some money of his own. Before that, he had spent some time working on construction at Camp Hood.

I kept thinking how I wished I had a job of my own. The only thing we got paid for while working on the farm was for picking cotton because the cotton could be sold, therefore making us some extra money. We could make a little more money by going to neighbors and relatives to pick cotton after we had finished picking our own crop.

I used all my cotton picking money to get new clothes for fall. My money would stretch a little further by buying material. Myrtice sewed a few dresses and skirts for me . She was good at sewing, and also made my cheer-leading uniform and my band costume. Mother ironed beautifully, so even though I didn't have many dresses, I was kept clean and pressed. Sometimes, I would talk my friends into swapping clothes at school, so that I would feel I had twice as many things to wear. Delores Patterson had some cute white boots that I loved to wear, especially when the band marched. When Dorothy

Maakestad got a new coat, she left her old one in her locker. I asked her if I could wear it since she no longer needed it. She was the preacher's daughter. We gave the preacher's family meat at hog killing time, as well as fruit and vegetables, so I figured it was a swap-off. However, Mother cleaned it and had me return it after a while.

I would swap lunches with anyone, so long as they didn't have biscuits. I had been taught to eat everything on my plate, but I'd start gagging and throwing up at the sight and smell of biscuits. Once I crawled under the bed and Myrtice and Noran pulled me out by my legs. After all my kicking and screaming, my parents gave up on trying to get me to eat biscuits.

Saturday mornings were usually set aside for washing several tubs of clothes and sheets. The afternoons were set aside for ironing. Sunday afternoon was always our day of rest. When we came home from church, we would usually be ready for a good meal. Our pressure cooker would often cook our meal while we were at church. The chicken or roast would be on one level and a couple of vegetables in compartments on the next level. We ate that along with the bread that Mother baked the day before. Ummmm, good!

Then we could sleep, read, or do whatever we wanted to, but we didn't have to work in the fields. In the evening, we did have our daily chores – milking cows, gathering eggs, carrying in wood, and slopping the hogs.

Friends I double-dated with were Fay Hastings, Delores Patterson, Connie Carlson, Frances Olson, and Neldine Rogstad. We went with the boys from Meridian one night and the boys from Clifton the next night. Noran and I had the same friends, so we often double-dated. If not, we'd often end up at the same place, which was usually at the Meridian Lake, where we danced for hours!

I still have a list of the first 106 guys that I went out with. Then I stopped writing the names down. Of course, that included my cousins, best friends, or anyone who would take me dancing or to a movie. Everyone at Cranfills Gap knew my main guy was Brady Cowan, but he was away at college part of the time before joining the U.S. Marines. Thank goodness, Brady was not domineering. He took me to his house when he came home on furlough, and told his mother that when he returns home from the war, he was going to ask me to marry him. We wrote many letters in the next two years. He told me he wouldn't ask me until after the war, because he didn't want me to sit at home all that time. What a guy!

My classmates, Bill and Barber, joined the Navy and Army Air Corps, respectively, before the end of the school year, because they wanted the service of their choice rather than wait to be drafted into the Army. So they didn't graduate with us, even though they did get their diplomas, (which were accepted by their mothers). The war was really getting fierce, and we said a prayer for them before the graduation ceremony began. Many of my cousins and friends were going into service. I wrote to all of them as it was our patriotic duty to keep their spirits up. They enjoyed hearing what was going on in their home town. Friends became very close to each other at this time and became like brothers and sisters.

My passion in high school was singing, dancing, reading, and telling jokes. We used to join friends and play, "Can you top this?" We would try to top each joke with a joke of our own.

I had been enduring pain in my right side for some time. Finally, the pain became so excruciating that the doctors told my parents to pack my side with ice and get me to the hospital the following morning. They took me to the Meridian Hospital and I was given a spinal injection. I said to the doctors, "This is great, a shot in my back, and I can just lie here awake and watch you operate on me by looking at that reflection around the light fixture". Then I told them a doctor joke. I don't know if they gave me a shot to knock me out, or if I passed out, but when I awakened, I was in my room minus my appendix. My mother was standing by my bed.

I had a cousin, Jesse Joel Olson, who lived in Meridian, and he could tell a joke like no one else. He should have been a stand-up comedian. Every day for a week he would come to the hospital to see me and tell jokes. It would hurt my side when I laughed, so I told him not to tell me any more jokes.

He would say that he could tell me one that was not so funny! But he had such a way of telling jokes, that I would start laughing before he got the joke told.

People had to have a sense of humor. We all went through some rough times during World War ll, and we had to laugh to keep from crying. Jesse was one of my first cousins to go into the service. He really looked sharp in his Navy uniform––blond curly hair and blue eyes. He made it through the war. We sat around him at a family reunion while he told us of some of his experiences. He was good at writing poetry, and I remember a couple of poems that were published in the Meridian Tribune.

Among other things that I enjoyed doing in high school and college was riding motorcycles. That was very exciting to me. My mother would have had a nervous breakdown had she ever seen me riding. I had several friends who had motorcycles, and it was so thrilling to go for a ride. Several of my friends were killed on their motorcycles, so that slowed me down. I've often agreed with the saying that young folks have more guts than sense!

I had two cousins, Truman and Wendell Pederson, whom I ran around with a lot through the years. Wendell and I went through

Clifton College together. He was a great quarterback in high school and college.

Truman and I went to North Texas State University together during the summer months. He had a car and we would go to movies, the library, and occasionally to McKinney or Dallas. We also ran with the same group in high school. He went into the Navy during the war. He married Laverne Cox when he finished college and I sang at their wedding. They had four beautiful children. I enjoyed watching them grow up and went to see them every time I went home to see Mother. Truman became a teacher, and also drove a school bus. When he retired, he moved to the farm, built a beautiful three-story house. After a few years he had a heart attack and died while attending to his goats.

Wendell was more like me than any of my cousins. He was always ready to let the good times roll! When he got out of the service, he worked in Fort Worth building airplanes. He also wrote the manuals used in production planning. He and JoNell had three beautiful and talented daughters.

On my dad's side, I had another cousin my age, Kenneth Surley, whom I always called my kissing cousin. He had been in the Navy during the war. When he came home he married Patricia, and they had two outstanding sons. Ken sold women's shoes at Neiman-Marcus while getting his education at Southern Methodist University in Dallas. After graduation, he became very successful in the insurance business.

Another cousin, Irvin Surley, was in the Army Air Corps during the war. He met a beautiful Norwegian girl, Ragnhild, while in Norway. After the war, they were married and he brought her back to Dallas. I remember her telling my dad that the Nygaard name was considered as royalty in Norway. Little is known about the immediate family in Norway. The mountains, forests, fjords, glaciers, and rivers provided a beautiful landscape. The people were also threatened by many hardships. Villages were built against a mountain or by the river's edge. Sometimes there were snow and mud slides that covered villages and killed many people.

My sister, Myrtice, has been to Norway three times and has done some research on the Nygaard family. She has been to the church in Norway where the Nygaards attended. She said the two front rows of seats were elevated and they had the VonKrog name carved into the end of the wooden seats. Further back, was a pew with the Nygaard name carved into it.

She was told that our great-great-grandfather had been the king of Norway for a short time and had decided to abdicate the throne, and be free of the responsibilities that caused threatening conflicts between Norway and Sweden. We don't know the entire story, as Dad said his family didn't discuss it. They were teachers, preachers, carpenters, cooks, and farmers, as there were on my mother's side of the family.

In recent years, we have been giving all the family heirlooms that our grandparents brought from Norway, to the Bosque County Museum in Clifton, Texas. All of our grandparents came over here in the 1880's.

My dad and his dad were both good carpenters. His dad made the trunks in which they brought their belongings when they came from Norway. One of the trunks is covered with caribou skin.

When people ask me if I am Norwegian, I tell them that I am a "thorough-bred Norwegian". However, I never had a desire to marry another Norwegian, or to learn the Norwegian language. I asked my mom about the necessity of learning to speak the language. She said I didn't have to learn another language if I didn't want to. She said her parents were told that they were in America now and should learn to speak the English language.

I had another language—it was called "slang" with a few cuss words thrown in once in a while. But I never used God's name in vain. I'm not that dumb! I don't want the wrath of God on me! But once in a while, the words, damn and hell seemed to be the only descriptive word I could think of that would express my thoughts.

I asked a cousin, Odessa, how things were going for her.

She said, "Well, I'll tell you! It seems that if it's not one damn thing, it's another!" I thought it was a funny expression, but by the time she told me all the things she had gone through in a few days, I couldn't think of any words myself that would be more fitting or better describe the circumstances.

Odessa's sister, Mardell, was in a wheel chair because of arthritis. When I asked her how she was, she replied, "Well, since you asked, I'll tell you! There are days when this arthritis gets so damn painful, that I wonder if it's going to kill me. Then there are other days when I wish to hell it would!"

(What better way could one explain the pain of arthritis?)

My biggest inspiration in life was my mother, Hannah. Instead of making me feel like I had to think like Myrtice and Noran, she let me feel that she was proud of me just the way I was. When I would ask her what I should do about certain things, she would say, "Whatever makes you happy, so just follow your heart."

She taught me by being a good example rather than criticizing me for what I did or how I thought. She let me be my "free-spirited" self, instead of trying to mold me into something I was not. We didn't have to say much as there was a mutual understanding between us. She was a quiet-natured little lady. Still waters run deep. Her good-natured thinking was that if you can't say anything good, don't say anything at all.

Mother never bragged about how smart she was. She was so quiet that most people didn't know, but my Aunt Minnie told me a lot of things about her. She said there were often spelling-bee parties at different peoples houses, and no one in the community could out-spell Mother.

Aunt Minnie and Mother went together to take their state test to qualify for a teaching certificate. Mother made the best score in Texas. Everything was 100 percent correct.

My cousin, Truman, often said she had the memory of an elephant. Mother could name all the states, all the presidents in the order that they held office, and could recite the Constitution of the United States before he had time to decide what he wanted for breakfast. Most of us learned the multiplication facts through the twelves, but I would ask her things like how much is 24 x 5 and she would instantly say 120. I asked how she could get it so fast and she would say by doubling. If 12 x 5 = 60, then 24 x 5 = 120. When I would go to church or to town with her, people would come up and say that she was the best teacher they ever had. Why was I not surprised?

Mother had unquestionable integrity, and was better and kinder than anyone I had ever known. If there was ever an angel on earth, she was it. She always make me proud. In her quiet way, she made an impact on those around her. My cousin Truman's son, Timothy, used to go by to see her when he was a young boy. He told me that on each visit, she would hold out to him three sticks of chewing gum, one each of Spearmint, Doublemint, and Juicy Fruit. He made his choice and was so happy. He loved her so much and was excited when his granddaughter was named Hannah. She is my mother's namesake!

I believe it was because of Mother's nature that I loved dogs so much. They could look into my eyes and knew how I felt. They would often remind me of Mother just by the way they would look at me, so trusting, so loving, and never judgmental.

After going to Bible school for two weeks every summer, and Sunday School all our lives, we still had two years of going to Bible Class on Saturday mornings before becoming confirmed in the Lutheran Church. That was fine with me, because it meant being with friends instead of having to work on the farm. We knew the Bible from front to back, knew most of the hymns, and had a little book called the Catechism that we memorized. On Confirmation Day, we sat in the choir seats in front of the congregation. When we were asked a question, we had to stand up and give the answer. I answered all my questions correctly. When we got home, I remember my dad putting his arm around my shoulder and telling me that he was very proud of me. It was the first time he had said that to me, and I almost cried. He wasn't mean, he just didn't show much affection in those days. He mellowed a lot in the many years that followed.

We all sang the Stamps Quartet songs on our five miles to church every Sunday. We had heard them on the radio and ordered their book.

We learned all their songs. Daddy sang in the male chorus, and we sang in the young adult choir. Noran and I sang some of the Stamps Quartet songs at the Junior Luther League on Sunday nights.

One night Noran sang "Paper Doll" on the PTA program. What he didn't know was that our minister, Reverand Maakestad, was to sing right before him. He had a powerful voice and sang a classical tune. You would have wondered if he sang in operas. We had a lot of laughs about it since then.

There is still an event so popular in Cranfills Gap that you have to make reservations months in advance to attend. It is the annual Lutefisk (codfish from Norway) Festival, held between the Thanksgiving and Christmas holidays. The ladies who serve, dress in the Native Norwegian Costumes.

The Rock Church of the Norwegian Lutheran Church, built in 1886, has been well-kept. It is located at the Cranfills Gap Cemetary, just a couple of miles east of town. Services at this historical landmark church are held for very special occasions. As I was growing up, there was a Norwegian service there on Sunday afternoons. My grandparents enjoyed going, since the sermon was preached in their language. I went with my parents, but only understood a few words.

Noran and I graduated from Cranfills Gap High School May 26, 1944. After we graduated and went back to our home room to remove our robes, I yelled out "Ok, everyone, I'll see you at the Lake in about fifteen minutes!"

Our home room teacher said, "Do you have time to pick up your diploma off my desk on the way out?"

In our excitement to get to Meridian Lake, we can't remember to this day, how our parents managed to get home that night without the car! It was a night to remember! Our graduating class went to Meridian Lake where we danced and celebrated the rest of the evening!

Norene and Myrtice in
their new grass skirts.
Next time, soldier
Send a top!

Noran shows off his
new army clothes

Norene and Noran
jitterbugging at the
Meridian Lake.

Otto & Hannah Nygaard

World War II song:
"You're in the army now;
You're not behind a plow.
You'll never get rich,
You son-of-a #*+*!
You're in the army now!

Noran in the Army

Harold--Norene--Noran--Avelyn
Double dating with my twin

Chapter 3

College, Driven to be Free

Noran and I graduated from high school in 1944, but we still didn't have definite plans for the future. As we were working on the farm that summer, who would drive up to our place but Coach Juel from the Clifton Junior College. (It was a small college supported by the Lutheran Church, and most of the students in our area went there to get their AA Degree.)

I'll guarantee you, we didn't look like college material. Noran was wearing a pair of blue jeans worn out at the knees. He was riding on a tractor. I looked even worse as I was wearing no shoes and was picking plums with Myrtice at the edge of the field. I hated wearing shoes, and still do! He came to invite us to Clifton College for the fall semester. We didn't know what to do.

Daddy had gone to West Texas to work in the fields, because he couldn't make enough money on the farm to justify staying there. Our fences were getting run down, and the sheep were getting into the fields faster than we could mend the fences. Daddy didn't seem to care what we did, so I suggested to Noran that we call a trucker, and send the sheep to Fort Worth to market. That's just what we did. We listened to the price of sheep on the radio at noon every day, so we picked a time when the market was better for selling.

Daddy seemed pleased that we sold the sheep at a fairly good price, so I suggested since we were not in any kind of trouble, why not sell the hogs, too. One thing led to another until we had sold all of them. The cows had plenty of water in the creek and grazed on the grassland, so they were not much trouble. We still had some chickens. We had always made a little grocery money selling eggs. We also ran our milk through a separator and sold the cream. By the end of the summer, we had eaten most of the chickens. What we didn't eat, Myrtice and Mother canned in the pressure cooker for the winter to use for soups.

We still didn't know whether we could afford to go to college (or even if we wanted to) but we knew our parents wanted us to go. Then Coach Juel came out the second time to talk with us about enrolling for the fall semester. We let him know we were thinking about it, and might give it a try. Even though we were not completely sold on the idea, I was thinking in the back of my mind that this might be the best chance we would ever have to get off the farm. I suggested to Noran that we drive to Clifton to find a house to rent that would be affordable. Well, between Mother having been a teacher and Myrtice starting out to become one, (she was just home for the summer) they managed to do some fast side-stepping to find a duplex for us to rent.

I told Mother that I would like for her to move in with us as there was no way I'd leave her on the farm by herself.

She said, "Oh, I hadn't thought of that." But I convinced her that we needed her to cook and iron for us. One of Mother's sisters lived in Clifton, and the other two were within ten miles and went to Clifton frequently to shop and visit with friends. They enjoyed quilting parties, and lunches together.

As luck would have it, since we had found a place to live, we drove to the college campus and signed up the same day! (I guess that was so we wouldn't change our minds before we got home!) As soon as we got home, we started packing our clothes, canned vegetables, and all those canned chickens!

Most people have their own agenda. IF YOU KEEP YOUR FAITH, IT'S EASIER TO KEEP YOUR FOCUS. ALWAYS TRY TO IMPROVE YOUR LIFE, BECAUSE POVERTY SUCKS THE HOPE OUT OF YOUR SOUL.

College was wonderful! My old friends were there, and I also made new friends. Noran and I had Daddy's old 1930 Model A Ford, and the kids would pile in and out of the car as we went to and from class.

There were several good night clubs in Waco (25 miles south) where we would all go dancing. If any of our cousins or friends got a furlough, you can be sure a big party was always planned, and a good time was had by all!

There's a saying, "Life may not be the party we asked for, but while we're here, we might as well dance."

We found college life to be great. I had my mother with us. Dad's job in West Texas stopped when the crops were brought in, so he went to Dallas and began working for an aircraft manufacturing plant. Later, he built streets and roads. This was a way to make extra money, and he had years of experience building roads while we were still living on the farm. He also had to put two of us through college, so he had to go where he could make some money.

One night, four of us friends decided to drive to Waco. On the way home, I mentioned to my friend, Joyce, that my mother would be worried if I didn't get home by midnight, so she speeded up. Suddenly, a tire blew out and she lost control of the car. The car flipped over into a ditch. Somehow, I flipped from the back seat to the front seat, and ended up on the floorboard between Joyce's knees. My date went from the back seat to the front and his head went through the front windshield. Both guys were unconscious.

A man (whom I later found out was the undertaker) from Valley Mills, saw us and pulled Joyce out first. Then he told me to put my arms up toward the window. It was then that I realized that I had a broken arm. He pulled me up and out of the car by the one arm that would move. He took us to a nearby farm house, and we stayed there while he called the ambulance in Clifton. We told him to take the boys first since we didn't know of their condition. Joyce had a cut on her head and arm. I had bruises on my face, back, along with a broken arm (I later found out that it was twisted half way off). She was in hysterics, but I was very calm, so I told them to take her first. She wouldn't go without me, so she was put in the front with the driver, and a man was in the back with me. The man knew my dad, and went to the same church in Clifton that I went to, so I felt comfortable with him. He asked what he could do to make me more comfortable, and I said it would help if he would hold his hand on my arm against my shoulder, so the rough ride wouldn't shake it so much. I was bleeding through a sweater and a wool jacket, so I was also getting a little weak.

Then I started praying the Lord's Prayer, and when I did, I saw a vision of Jesus with His arms stretched toward me. There were angels on each side of Him. I felt very happy and calm.

I said to the man, "I can see Jesus and some angels. They are right above us – look!" When I said "look" the vision vanished. Then I passed out, and didn't wake up again until I was in a hospital room with my brother and mother by my side.

I asked about the others and was told they would all be okay. I also noticed that my new suit and sweater had been cut off of me. My friends were out of the hospital after a couple of days, but I had to stay there for over a week. I suppose my arm had become tangled in the steering wheel, and I had a double compound fracture. The doctors had never had a patient with a break like mine, and were not sure they could save my arm, so I had to sign a paper that they could do what they could do–with no guarantee. They later told me they called two other doctors while they were setting it—one from Dallas and one from Oklahoma.

Noran came the next day with a big 14-inch white curley stuffed dog that he won at the Halloween Carnival the night before. That dog gave me a lot of comfort in the days ahead. Noran held up a tablet for me to write a note to Daddy.

I wrote, "Don't worry about me—remember, I'm a good lefty!" He mailed it and Daddy got it the next day. As soon as Daddy got it, he called his boss and said he needed to take a day off. One side of my face was black, from my half shut eye to my jaw. When the nurse opened the door, Daddy started crying. I kept telling him that I would be okay. Later that day, he had to go back to Dallas, and asked what he could do to make me comfortable. My face itched (I suppose from some kind of medicine), so I asked if he would wipe my face with a damp cloth until I went to sleep. He did it – ever so gently.

My doctors told me that they thought I was the bravest patient they had ever had in that hospital because I was so calm and strong. I knew it was because of my visit with Jesus Christ. But I figured that if I told anyone of my experience, they would probably tell me that I was nuts or that I had a great imagination. Even the Clifton Record Newspaper had the article written up as a miracle that we all got out alive.

A hospital bed was sent to our house, and I had to sleep sitting up for six more weeks. My cousin, James Anderson, told me that he had gone to see the car hauled off as junk, and said that the speedometer got stuck at 100 miles per hour.

I had missed quite a lot of schooling, and the teachers offered to let me take my test orally. I said that I would rather take the test with the class , and with my left hand. By now, I was ambidextrous. In fact, I was rather enjoying doing things with my left hand, and told my friends that I was glad it was my right arm, instead of the left one that was broken.

When I got to North Texas University in Denton, I did some research on visions. The books explained that visions are meant for that one person, and if anyone else was called upon to look, the vision would vanish. That satisfied me to know that I wasn't knocked crazy—that I really did see Jesus and I have thought about that moment many times since then.

I remember that someone famous (but I can't remember who) said as he was dying, "If this is death, then it is much easier than life."

By the end of the mid-term semester, Noran got that famous "I WANT YOU" letter from Uncle Sam. I believe this was the saddest point in my life, as being twins, we had been inseparable. It was just as hard on my parents and sister, but we weren't brought up to be cry-babies, so we knew we had to accept it, and pray the war wouldn't last much longer. We always tried to make the best of a bad situation, so we had a farewell party at Aunt Lizzie's house in Clifton. Our relatives were there for lunch and picture taking. Most of our cousins were already in service.

I will always remember walking with Noran to the train station on the day of his departure. Several of his friends left at the same time. We had many friends and acquaintances who had been killed in service , so we were aware that saying good-bye might really mean "good-bye".

As I walked home, it started raining very lightly. As I turned my face up toward the sky, it was as though Heaven was crying in my face. People who have a twin probably understand that bond that I am referring to. It was as though half of me was going to war.

My friend, Sarah Knudson, suggested we sign up to be cadet nurses. I told her that it would probably do my family in for two of us to be gone at the same time. I liked the idea, and agreed to take some human physiology classes with her, and once I satisfied my family with a college degree, perhaps we could swing it.

I liked all my teachers, but I'll never forget Coach Juel and Mrs. Pierson. I looked forward to their classes each day because they made learning interesting, and showed so much love and compassion to all of us, who sometimes felt lost or misunderstood.

I remember while at Clifton Junior College, Coach Juel asked me to pitch in a girl's softball team. I wasn't a great ball player, but I liked the game better than any other sport. I even had a Ted Williams baseball glove.

I said, "Please, Coach, don't ask me to pitch!"

He said, "Why not?"

I said, "Because no one likes batting off a left-handed pitcher, and besides that, they will call me 'lefty', 'south-paw', and Lord only knows what else!"

"Good!" he said, "That's why I want you out there, lefty! Let's play ball!"

After teaching physical education for fifteen years in Dallas and also at the Space Center (Houston), I put my Ted Williams glove in a garage sale. I hope that whoever has it remembers what an icon he was, and how he loved this country and the game of baseball. Ted Williams died on July 5, 2002 at the age of 83.

One night, Brady's mother came walking up to our house from town. She was living in Fort Worth, and had come by bus 100 miles to let me know that Brady had been killed on Iwo Jima. He had been a schoolmate and I had liked him since I was in the sixth grade, and here I was in college. Dreams for the future were completely crushed. I knew I would never find anyone like him, and I still often think about him. I threw myself across the bed and cried and cried. The war was horrible! So many of my friends were being killed.

I remember going to the post office, and in one day, had twenty-one letters returned to me! Life was a nightmare! But we had to keep going. We were patriotic and did everything to help win the war. My favorite charity has always been to the military service. In my heart, I give in memory of Brady, and all my friends who went through World War ll.

I knew from that day on that my life would be different. I had no idea how to plan my future, but I realized some time later that God would direct me.

To everything, there is a season; a time for every purpose under heaven: a time to weep, a time to laugh, a time to mourn, and a time to dance.

~ Ecclesiastes 3:1,4

What I am most proud of in this world is to be an American citizen. My regret is that I did no service for my country, but I honor those who fought to make this a great country. The war was coming to an end at the time I was old enough to join anything. There were not many women in service during the World War ll days either, but they worked in factories and did many things to help win the war. We made many sacrifices and were rationed in gas, sugar, and many other commodities. We felt it was our patriotic duty to write to all the friends, especially those from our home town, to let them know what was happening in their community, and to let them know we were proud of them.

I am so proud of those who sacrificed their time (and for many, their lives), for all of us who live in this great country. I believe that these people , especially those who have been in active duty, should never have to want for anything for the rest of their lives. They were ordinary people who did extraordinary things to make this country great.

Listening to the Star-Spangled Banner and other patriotic songs always brings tears to my eyes. I love this country beyond belief. War is a terrible thing for these young people to go through, and I imagine it takes a lot of faith in God to be able to go through such an ordeal. Then they have to come home and forgive their enemies to be able to go on with their lives.

Many wouldn't talk about their experiences, but I would encourage everyone to write about them and pass it down for future generations.

This would be a good project for everyone to do, whether you were in service or not. All of us have a combination of happiness, sorrow, defeat, triumph, but something within us gives us the wisdom to go on in spite of short-comings, and by the grace of God, know that each has done his best under the prevailing circumstances. Most of us have to struggle through many things – as Frank Sinatra would sing, "That's Life".

During my second year of college, I was in the Christmas Pageant. (I was always an angel in the Christmas pageants, if you can imagine!) I had a speaking part, as well as a singing part. I was suffering from the flu and got out of bed to attend the play practice the day before our performance. The teacher was grateful for my attending the practice and the program while in my condition. I suppose neither of us thought about spreading the flu germ to the rest of the group. I just knew the program wasn't going to be ruined because of my illness. I always had "the show must go on" attitude.

The service men started coming home at the end of the war. We celebrated by hitch-hiking to the Meridian Lake for a big dance. Joy Cole, Regina Smith, Connie Carlson, and I had dresses made alike with a full skirt with a mid-riff top. Strange as it may seem, the guy who picked us up was the same undertaker who helped me the night we were in the car wreck. He recognized me and jokingly told me that he thought he had a big business coming in that night. (Hitch-hiking in those days were not the same as it is today. Life was much safer then and we all knew everyone.)

During the second year of college some of the servicemen from Clifton began returning home. They enrolled in college under the U.S. Government bill, which paid for their education.

During that same time, the English Department put on a play called, "Pride and Prejudice". I played the part of Lydia, the wild one, who thought only of having a good time! Why was I not surprised when the teacher told me I would be perfect for the part? What a hoot it turned out to be!

We worked on the play for about six weeks and had practice at night twice a week. We had rented costumes from a place in Dallas, but we had never practiced in them. Our dresses had hoop petticoats underneath. When one girl was supposed to sit down, her hoop raised up her dress, for all to see! She tried to push it down, but it kept popping up. Meanwhile, I went into laughing hysterics! I was supposed to be crying, so I put my hankie over my face, (instead of just my eyes) and continued laughing. By now, the entire audience was laughing. Finally, the teacher had to go out on the stage and show her how to lift the hoop slightly before sitting down.

As if that wasn't enough, the guy who played the part of my boyfriend, was one of the returned servicemen. Unfortunately, some of them drank, and when he came out on the stage, he grinned and said, "Well, hello, Lydia!"

As he jokingly slapped me across the shoulder, I could smell liquor on his breath, and anyone who took one look at him knew he was drunk.

I glanced at the teacher behind the curtains and when I saw the worried look on her face, I again went into laughing hysterics. I tried to stop laughing by remembering that people had paid to see our play, but the more I tried to stop, the worse I got. It was quite obvious by now that everyone knew he was drunk and staggering all over the stage. But the audience seemed to have enjoyed the play in more ways than one.

I had been taking a tumbling course at this time, also. I was fairly good in sports. One night, as we walked home from play practice, I was playing leap frog with one of the guys. Each time, I told him to get higher. Suddenly, he was afraid I couldn't make it, so he squatted down just as I got ready to push against his back. Since his back was not there to push on, I tumbled over him, head first, hitting the cement.

I broke my left arm, this time at the shoulder. My friends asked if I was all right.

I started laughing as I said, "No, but at least I don't need an ambulance." This happened right in front of the hospital. When I got home, I told Mother that I had bought us both some aspirin because I had broken my arm.

While I was on the mend, a couple of guys came by and asked if I could ride a horse. I told them they were talking to a country gal. I rode them bareback on the farm, but they were old, slow horses. I jumped on and this horse gave me the ride of my life! He bucked and ran, and I finally got him turned around. This was not an easy task as one of my arms was still in a sling. Just as I got home, the horse ran under a tree and a limb hit me right above my eye.

It really scared my mother, because she was afraid I had lost my eye. The guy then told me he had started the day before to break the horse for riding. There was a popular saying at the time, "Do you dare to be different?" It didn't take much for me to dare to do anything.

A couple of weeks later, four of the guys were planning to drive to Fort Worth to enroll in Texas Christian University for the next semester . They asked Regina and me if we wanted to ride up there with them. As luck would have it, we had a test scheduled that day, so we couldn't go. The teachers had become quite lenient with the students since the service men had come back home—but we were never to skip on a test day. The four friends were driving too fast and failed to make a turn. They were thrown out of their convertible and killed. There were four funerals in our town that week. What a sad time for our little town and all the friends and families.

The guys who came back from service did add a little spice to our classes. Teachers had a way of being disturbed when we whispered in class, so our recourse was to pass notes to each other. One morning, I was ten minutes late to class. On the opposite side of the room, sat the preacher's son (just back from service). About six people helped get his note passed to me which read, "If you had any last night, SMILE!" As I have said before, any time I try not to laugh, I go into laughing hysterics! The teacher pointed to the door, so I walked out, and sat in the library until the next class. I know some of my readers think I must have a twisted mind, but wouldn't anyone have laughed getting an unexpected note like that from a preacher's kid? Have we lost our sense of humor? (I think Mother Theresa would have laughed.)

It's a wonder I wasn't thrown out of my classes daily. I was always writing notes and laughing. Our elderly Bible teacher read us the story about God telling Abraham to saddle up his ass, hit the road, and take his son, Isaac, with him! I somehow found that to be funny. I figured if God didn't want us to laugh, He would have used the word DONKEY.

As the service men came home, there was a lot of drinking. We were just out of high school so we stayed clear of them, but we were amused at some of their antics. Word on the street was that a couple of them got drunk in Waco and the next morning there was a 5-foot "Rainbow Girl" at the entrance to the campus. (The logo for the Rainbow Bakery was a "rainbow girl".) She had a loaf of bread under her arm, and she was placed as though she were walking to school. In the afternoon, someone would turn her around, as though she were leaving the campus. Her dress was red on one side and blue on the other side. The guys had also stolen a bench, so we could sit and visit with friends. After a few days, she and the bench disappeared from the campus.

In one of my Education classes, I went to the Clifton Elementary School to teach a second grade class twice a week for an hour. I had also taught them some songs and poems. At the end of the semester we presented a program at the college. Their parents were there, so I was pleased that the students did such a good job. As the curtain closed, the teacher asked me to step in front of the curtain and say something to the parents.

For a split second, I froze. I took a deep breath and went out and said, "Thanks for coming to our program. We hope you have enjoyed it as much as we have enjoyed presenting it to you."

After the program, my teacher, Mrs. Pierson told me she thought I would make an excellent teacher. I don't know what she saw in me to think I would become a great teacher. I know many others who would have voted me least likely to become a teacher.

After two years of college, I still wasn't sure what I wanted to do with my life. A few days later one of the little second grade boys was hit in the temple, with a baseball, and went into a coma and died that night. It seemed that between the war and accidents, there was so much death to deal with.

The day after we graduated from Clifton College, my friend, Sarah Knudson, (who wanted to be a cadet nurse) was struck by lightning as she finished mowing the yard. Her mother had called and told her the weather was getting stormy and that she had better stop mowing. But she called back and told her mother that she was almost finished, and besides, she wasn't afraid. Her death was another big shock to many of us. She had lived on the farm next to us, and had also brought her parents with her to college. They lived in a little house on the campus, and her dad became the custodian of the college.

After the funeral, Myrtice was getting ready to go to North Texas University in Denton. She asked me to come and be her roommate. Mother wanted me to continue with my education, so I went. Mother knew all her neighbors and didn't mind living alone.

Tommy Taylor
Take me out to the ball game

Frank Belinski
We almost married

Mr. Simpson

Mrs. Milling

Miss Nygaard

Aunt Katie

Noran

Chapter 4

My First Teaching Job - The Abundant Life

World War II had finally come to an end. President Roosevelt died a few months earlier, and Harry Truman finished out his term of office. He was referred to as "Give em' hell, Harry!" President Truman ran for another term and won.

This undoubtedly is a fictitious story but it goes like this: In the 1948 Presidential Election, after which Harry S. Truman had defeated Governor Thomas E. Dewey, Mr. Truman sent Mr. Dewey a note in the form a poem which read:

Let by-gones be by-gones,

Let the bitterness pass;

I'll hug your elephant

You can kiss my donkey.

When the summer was almost over, Randall Simpson, the school superintendent at Strawn, Texas, went to Clifton College to recruit potential teachers. He was formerly our coach at Cranfills Gap High School. He told me later that my name was the first one mentioned and repeated for references in his quest for a teacher. He said he drove another 150 miles to find me in Denton. After a pleasant interview, I told him I would go there the following weekend to see how I felt about going to work in Strawn.

Edwin and Bea Larson from McKinney, took Myrtice and me there and we all liked it. Strawn had once been a coal mining town. We took several pictures from the top of an old coal mine. Mother's parents had lived in the area when they first arrived from Norway and my grandfather worked in the coal mines for several years. It was now a small town and I liked it. I decided to accept the teaching position.

I lived with Mrs. Milling, who was the principal of the Strawn Elementary School. Mr. Simpson was in the high school building but I saw him often.

I remember so well the first month of teaching the second grade. I had just graduated from Clifton Junior College with a pretty wild bunch of classmates. My new job was so over-whelming, that I wondered if I could handle it. There were so many things to learn at once. One day, as I was writing something on the blackboard for the class to copy, one of the pupils asked me a question. In my frustration, I answered back, "HELL NO".

I turned red as one child said, "What did you say, Miss Nygaard?"

I slowly turned around and said, "Well, no !"

Of course, the children were laughing and so was I, because I knew, they knew, and God knew, they heard me correctly the first time! This happened on a Friday, and I wondered all weekend whether or not I would have a room of angry parents on Monday morning. And even worse, I wondered if they would talk to the superintendent or principal and get me fired.

All weekend, I prayed to God that He would get me out of one more mess! I also asked Him to keep His hands over my mouth until I realized that I was teaching the future leaders of America! Believe me, times were quite different in 1946 than they are today. Thank God, He came to my rescue and the incident never came up.

Mrs. Milling and I got along beautifully. What an exciting time in my life! I finally had my very own job! The people in that community were Polish, and they loved to dance. I learned the Polka and Schottische dances from them. When the weather was cold or rainy and we couldn't go outside to exercise, we would open our classroom doors to a wide hall and each class had their own area in which to dance. We also taught a few square dances like, "Texas Star" and "Marching Through Georgia".

I loved this place. It was about the same size as Cranfills Gap, but with a different attitude. We couldn't even have a senior dance at our high school, and here we were dancing at school every time we had a rainy day schedule.

Even at one of the PTA meetings, they called me to come up to the stage. We formed a Conga Line, and played a game using popular tunes. They would just play a little of the tune and if the leader of the line didn't know the tune, he would have to sit down. I knew every popular tune out there, so there was no way I could lose. I tied with another guy who also knew all the tunes, because he owned the beer joint down town, and had those nickelodeons attached to all the tables, by the music selector boxes that played popular tunes. His daughter was one of my pupils. I couldn't wait to tell my friends in Cranfills Gap that I danced at a PTA program with the bar owner. Cranfills Gap was a dry town.

One day, I told my principal, Mrs. Milling, that the banker's son had invited me to a dance for the following Saturday night, and it was going to be at the city hall downtown. I asked her if I would be in trouble if I went to the dance.

She said, "Norene, if you don't go, you will be the only one in town not there!"

She was right. Not only were the parents there but the children were there having a good time dancing, too. Wow! I knew that Strawn was my kind of town. There were many little towns around there which also had their little honky tonks, so I was having the time of my life!

I enjoyed sports, so sometimes in the afternoons, I'd put on a pair of shorts and show the high school boys that I could jump as high and as far as they could. Mr. Simpson asked if I would take some of the kids to the County Interscholastic League. That was fun for me as I had played softball, volley ball, and tennis when I was in high school. I went with them on a bus to Ranger.

For a while, I played on a women's softball team at night. I decided to drop out when the doctor of the town asked me to do some secretarial work for him after school. I would post payments, make appointments, and answer the phone. This gave me a chance to make a little extra money so I could go back to college during the summer.

GOD GIVES US MANY TALENTS. ALL WE HAVE TO DO IS FIND OUR PASSION, AND FOCUS ON IT. Passion is dedication to an ideal, and the determined pursuit of that ideal. For me, it is an obsession with an attitude. To have my own job was a lifetime dream. To have two jobs at a time was sensational. I thought I could move mountains!

Within the space of five years, I had finished four years of college and three years of teaching. By going to college during the summer, taking correspondence courses during the winter, I saved two years of what I would have called "wasting time". That is why I told people I "sweated blood" to get my degree.

Myrtice and I were roommates during the summers in Denton. She was working on her M.A. degree while I worked on my B.S. degree. We spent many weekends in McKinney with Edwin and Bea Larson. They planned many fun times for us. Sometimes, we would spend the weekend fishing at the lake. They would often rent a lake house that would sleep over twenty people. This permitted a group of people to have a good time with relatives and friends. Other times, they would take us to the Starlight Operetta at Fair Park in Dallas. There were also weekends when Myrtice and I would double-date. She dated Curtis Larson whom she later married, and I went with different guys who were his friends.

There were also guys on the campus whom I dated. One guy was the drummer of the North Texas Band and he drove a big blue Cadillac convertible. He was a good looking American Indian. I met another American Indian at the library where I spent many hours. He was from Oklahoma. What I didn't know was that they were fraternity brothers.

One evening, unknowingly to me, they both decided to come together to pick me up for a date, even though I only had a date with one of them. We drove to Fort Worth to eat ribs at a barbecue restaurant. Through their jealous behavior they tried to make me feel uncomfortable. It didn't bother me because I didn't feel that serious about either of them. I was just there for the summer. Before the night was over they were practically fighting each other. Needless to say, I never saw them again, but I wouldn't have allowed myself to get involved with someone jealous anyway, because I liked going out with many different guys.

When Myrtice and I were at North Texas University the last summer before we graduated, we both needed a required course in science, so we signed up for a chemistry class. We saw from the beginning that we were in trouble. We had no earthly idea what the teacher was trying to convey to us. As we were about to leave for the weekend, we saw a man from the Administration Building. He asked what we were up to and we told him we were leaving town and were not sure we should bother to come back. We explained that we were afraid we were going to fail chemistry and we were quite concerned since neither of us had a failing grade, and more importantly, we were hoping to graduate at the end of the summer. Myrtice was working on her Masters Degree at the same time I was working on my Bachelors Degree.

He said, "Don't you know you have to go to the old codger's Sunday School Class to pass? Everyone does it!" He even gave us an outline of his lesson. We not only had a lot of religious training as children, but both of us had taken two years of Bible study when we were in Clifton Junior College.

So we walked into his Sunday School class with much confidence. Sure enough, the entire class was there, and had supposedly been going every Sunday. As he asked the questions, Myrtice would answer one question and I would answer the next one. No one else had a chance to answer, because we raised our hands before he had finished the question.

We felt so proud of ourselves until Monday morning when he stood before the class and said, "I must say, if certain people were as smart in chemistry class as they are on the Bible, they wouldn't have to come to my Sunday School Class to pass!"

Of course, everyone turned to look at us, as our faces turn beet red. We felt about as big as two little piss-ants! Until the grades came out, we were not sure if we would graduate. We both passed, so we invited all our family and friends to the graduation ceremony so they could see that we made it! However, don't ask me to tell you in one sentence what I learned in chemistry that summer of '49. (I made a C, and was proud of it!)

I had also taken an elective course in Voice, thinking that it would be an easy way to bring up my grade average. After I had begun, I found out that I bit off more than I could chew. For the final test, they gave each of us a piece of music and told us to sing it the next day. I have never claimed that I could read music that well, but I had an ear for music. If I could hear the tune one time, I could sing it. I asked a friend to play it on the piano for me. I had it! The next day, I saw a friend from Clifton and he looked like he was sick.

I asked him what was wrong and he said he had to take his final in a few minutes. I wondered how he could have been worried, as I had heard him sing at many funerals and weddings. I told him not to worry because he was as good as they get.

He said, "Do you realize that people come here from all over the country, because of the reputation that the Music Department has?" We were all standing in the vestibule outside the classroom waiting to be called in.

I thought to myself, "What was I thinking about when I signed up for this course? If he is worried, then I'm doomed!"

About then, I was called in to sing. You guessed it! When I'm nervous, I laugh. Well, I started singing, and made it through two or three lines and then went into laughing hysterics!

The three judges asked me what was so funny and I explained what had happened outside the door with this excellent singer from my hometown. I explained that I took the course just for fun as an elective, and had no goals for becoming a professional singer. We all had a good laugh, as I told them I was glad to have taken a voice course from the institution where the best in the country come to get their training. I still managed a pretty good grade, but not an A.

This uncomfortable laughter was perhaps a reaction from my years of confusion with the handedness problem. But at last I was getting an understanding and control of the situation which had been such a problem in my earlier years.

I had finally learned to rise above my problem by becoming ambidextrous, giving me a different attitude. I decided that there are advantages to being ambidextrous. HE WHO USES ONLY ONE HAND OR ONE LEG TO DO THINGS IS NO BETTER OFF THAN SOMEONE WHO HAS ONLY ONE HAND OR ONE LEG.

You should see me drive a car. I have my right foot on the accelerator and my left foot on the brake. I can stop on a dime! I use both hands for a lot of things. I write right-handed, but color, draw, or use the eraser left-handed.

I cut my steak with my left hand and use my fork in my right hand to transfer food to my mouth. This eliminates changing hands back and forth.

I throw a ball left-handed, but bat right-handed. But in many things, I do as well with one hand as I do with the other. When I'm alone, I usually eat left-handed.

While in Strawn my first year, I met a good-looking guy, Tommy Taylor, who was playing on a semi-professional baseball team. We had limited time together as I was working two jobs, and he was working hard to become a professional baseball player.

When summer came, I went back to North Texas University in Denton to continue working toward my degree. At the end of the semester, I went to Interlochen, Michigan as a Lutheran student representative from North Texas University. It was a beautiful music camp, but we used it as a summer Bible Camp. We had some good times during the day playing softball, swimming, or other sports. In the evenings, we would break up into group meetings. Each morning, we started the day with a prayer and a short service. Then we had breakfast, and started a full day of various activities. I arrived back in Strawn just in time for the school year to begin.

In my spare time, I took a correspondence course in Children's Literature from Abilene Christian College. As I got dressed to go to the Palo Pinto Court House to take a test on the course that I was completing, I was listening to the morning news on the radio. I was shocked to hear that my cousin, Jesse Joel Olson had been struck and killed by a car as he was hitch-hiking from the navel base in Grand Prairie to Fort Worth where he lived. Mrs. Milling took me to Palo Pinto so I could take my test. Then I caught a bus and went home. Noran was in West Texas and had also heard the news and caught the bus home. He changed buses in Fort Worth and happened to get on the same bus with Jesse Joel's ex-wife, who had come from Kansas to attend Jesse's funeral.

In my second year of teaching in Strawn, I got word from Mother that Mrs. Cowan had Brady's body sent home from Iwo Jima, and his funeral would be that weekend. I bought a new black suit, gray shoes, bag, and hat.

I placed the Marine Emblem which Brady had sent to me, on my shoulder. His mother and dad asked me to sit with them and their other son, Bonley. This was a very sad time of my life. I knew I would never meet anyone who could compare with Brady.

But that's life! Another weekend, his parents asked me to come to Fort Worth. They gave me all the letters that I had written to Brady. They had been sent back with his belongings. They also gave me one of his hats and another Marine emblem. Bonley, (whom I called Bud) and I went roller skating that afternoon before he took me back to Strawn. I never saw his parents again, as they both died. Bonley had lost his brother, mother, and dad and the emotional strain required his going to Glen Rose for therapy. Noran and I located him a few years ago and had a good visit with him. I heard he had died in February of 2006.

The third year that I taught in Strawn, I met a very nice guy named Frank Belinski. He was a good dancer and we had some good times. I liked him, but decided I would go to Dallas to see what I thought of the city life. He followed me and put an engagement ring on my finger, but it didn't stay long. He suggested I give up my job and have a bunch of children. I didn't go four years to college to have children. I was not about to give up my job. So I returned the ring, and told him that I didn't like to wear rings because I heard engagement rings cut off circulation. My motto has always been, "NEVER GIVE UP ANYTHING YOU HAVE UNLESS YOU CAN EXCHANGE IT FOR SOMETHING BETTER".

I had taught three years in Strawn. When I graduated from North Texas University in 1949, I had an urge to find out all about the excitement of living in the city. My cousin, Truman Pederson, who was in North Texas for the summer, took me to Dallas to apply for a job with the Dallas Independent School District.

I went to see Dr. Walker, who was the Assistant Superintendent of the Dallas Independent School System.

As I walked in, I said, "I hear you are Doak Walker's dad." (The famous football player)

He smiled and gently said, "Let's put it this way, Doak is my son."

We laughed, and I immediately felt comfortable with him. He hired me on the spot.

Before I moved to Dallas, Noran had returned from the Armed Services. We decided to go to Dallas to take Daddy and his sister, Katie, out on the town with us. We all caught a street car and went downtown. Noran picked up a little bottle of bourbon on our way to the night club. We each had one little drink, and the stripper danced up to our table. She was the famous Candy Barr.

One of Dad's friends with whom he worked, had joined us and offered to drive us home. It was a little late to catch the street car. That guy was full of jokes, and he finished one of them as he walked us up to my aunt's door. He had us laughing hysterically.

About that time, her daughter, Martha, opened the door, and said, "Good grief, Mother, quit being so loud. The neighbors are going to think we have a bunch of drunks on the front porch!"

That made us laugh again, so Aunt Katie said, "Martha, we're just having a good time. What's wrong with that?"

The next day, as we were having lunch at Aunt Katie's house, Dad said that he was proud of us. We all found that one drink was enough, and we all had a good time. That was the first time we had ever attempted to sip on anything in front of my dad. I was also proud of my dad because he saw that we were grown, yet in control of ourselves.

All my relatives were fun to be around. Aunt Katie had a laugh that I enjoyed hearing. It sounded like she was saying, "hee, hee, hee, hee, hee!"

From about 1940 to 1955 were the years known to me as the "Dance Hall Days", and those were the greatest years in musical history. We enjoyed the "Big Band Music" with leaders such as Benny Goodman, Harry James, Tommy Dorsey, Glen Miller, and Artie Shaw. Any time they came within a reasonable distance, I would see that arrangements were made for us to go dancing.

Norene-- as a hair model

Bennie Kelly-Coach at Long Jr. High. We went together and worked the city parks for 3 years.

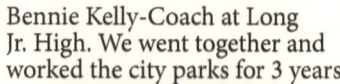

The Rev. Miller Cragon

Robert Speegle, M.D.

Frank DeVera and Norene

Ann Priest

India Ann Priest
(Punkin)

Norene

Myrtice

Ann Priest--Part owner of DeVera Dance Studio
Director of John Robert Powers Modeling Schools

Frank DeVera

Lord, if you can't make me better, don't worry about it--
I'm having a real good time like I am!

Ronnie Shipman

A whole lot of shakin'
goin' on!

Chapter 5

Hello Dallas! Let the Good Times Roll

Hello Dallas, Texas! I couldn't pack fast enough to find a place to live near the school in Oak Cliff where I had been assigned to teach. It happened that John Reagan Elementary was the same school where my cousins, Clarence, Martha, and Kenneth attended when they were children. My Aunt Katie lived only two or three blocks from the school. Daddy had lived with her for a while when he first moved to Dallas, but now he had an apartment across the street. I met both of them every Sunday at the Oak Cliff Lutheran Church. My aunt often invited my dad and me to have lunch with Uncle Oscar and her on Sundays.

Aunt Katie took me "under her wing" and helped me become a city gal. She was a furrier downtown making fur coats. She knew the three Aaron brothers who owned a women's wholesale clothing store downtown. She introduced me to them, and they let me buy my clothes at their wholesale prices. I bought cashmere coats, cashmere sweaters, many sun dresses, and cocktail dresses. Wow! A dream come true! Aunt Katie made her daughter a new fur jacket, and gave me her old one. I was so thrilled to have a real fur jacket!

She jokingly said, "I hope Martha doesn't come home some weekend and wonder where her old fur jacket is."

I loved Dallas! I loved teaching the second grade! I felt like I was sitting on top of the world! I would often get on the streetcar and go downtown.

It was fun and only cost six cents to ride! I went in and out of all the big stores on Saturdays, especially when they were having some big sales. There were also many stores in Oak Cliff, so shopping became a favorite way of spending the weekends.

One night a week, I'd catch a streetcar and go downtown to a modeling school for self-improvement and for something to do. I had no intention of getting a job out of this, but by accident, I became a hair model. I once worked at the "Texas Convention for Hair Styles" at the Baker Hotel. Another time, my hair was styled on television by Michael, who owned a beauty shop. Another owner, John Basden, who had a shop in Oak Lawn, had pictures of my hair style in his salon window. This led to my being chosen as one of the contestants in the "Miss Flame of Dallas" contest sponsored by the Dallas Firemen. My hair was red at the time.

My brother recently asked what my title was when the firemen chose me. My sister and were both having one of those "senior moments" and couldn't remember, so she told him that I was chosen as "The Last of the Red Hot Mamas!"

Meanwhile, I was making my mark in the teaching profession. The Dallas Morning News sponsored a contest for the most outstanding teachers in Dallas. Believe it or not, I was in the top five chosen as winners. The PTA at John Reagan School had written a letter about why they thought I was the most outstanding teacher. Instead of the principal giving me the plaque, she hung it in her office. I was proud of the honor, even though I didn't get to take the plaque with me. I knew that my mother, who had been a teacher for seven years before she married, would be proud of me. I was also offered a trip to be an exchange student at the Oxford University in England for the summer. However, I was having the time of my life in Dallas, so I didn't want to leave Dallas.

Instead, I went down to the Dallas School Administration Building and asked Dr. Walker if he could transfer me to another school. I told him that I had a high respect for my principal. She had invited me to go to church with her and I went. However, I felt that I was walking on egg shells at school.

I smiled and spoke to the children as they came into my room. She came into my room and told my class that she didn't want to hear a locker close, and she did not want to hear them speak to me. They were to come into the building and go directly to their desk. She didn't want to hear a sound. They were not to open their mouths nor were they to go to the rest room, except right before lunch and recess.

In the old days, learning was made easier than it is today. Children were taught standards and discipline. It wasn't a matter of "no child left behind." It was "learn or expect a sore behind." There are many ways to make learning easy and fun.

We were people, not robots! My methods of teaching were so different from the "never smile, never speak" attitude that I observed from her.

Dr. Walker, of course, knew her and understood my situation. Without asking further questions, he said that he would have me transferred.

I was going with a physical education teacher, Bennie Kelly. He was half- Indian and half-Irish. We both got jobs for the summer working for the Dallas City Parks and Playgrounds. We did this for three years. I needed a job and I liked the challenge. One summer, we took the kids to camp for the last two weeks of the summer. I had the girls and Bennie had the boys, who were on the other side of the fence! It was fun though. We had arts and crafts, swimming, and softball from morning until night.

The following fall I went to another school, the L.O. Donald Elementary, and taught the fourth grade. During the many years of teaching in the classroom, we often had "show and tell". It was a way for the children to interact with their classmates, as well as gaining confidence for public speaking.

One morning, Johnny got in front of the class and said, "I really don't have anything to show, but I would like to tell you a story my uncle told me.

He was in World War ll, and when the planes came over, the 'ack-acks' shot the HELL out of them!"

I said, (in shock) "The WHAT?" (By now, the class was laughing)

He said, "The 'ack-acks'; you know, the anti-aircraft." He still didn't know why everyone was laughing, so a little boy ran up and whispered in his ear.

He just smiled a little and said, "Well anyway,"(and went on with his story.)

Another day, one of the fourth grade boys said, "Miss Nygaard, our Social Studies book shows an entire chapter on each of the first three presidents, while none of the others were even mentioned. They were not any more important or did more than any of the other presidents, did they?"

This was an election year and the "Democrats" and "Republicans" were already sitting at separate tables in the lunch room.

I jokingly said, "Well, they did more than President Truman, didn't they?"

The class laughed as I tried to explain that perhaps they aren't expected to learn about all of them in one semester. I promised to bring some library books for them to read about some of the other presidents; even though they might be written for a higher level. Suddenly, I noticed a boy pass a note across the aisle to his friend. I walked by and picked it up. Then I made the mistake of opening it in front of the class.

He had written, "I think President Truman is a turd, don't you?"

I wasn't expecting anything like that. You guessed it, I started laughing as I walked out of the room. The other fourth grade teacher saw me as I left the room laughing. I had a small office next door, and she came in and read my note and she also started laughing. We were saved by the recess bell! She went back and dismissed our classes to go outside. We had our laugh and then went downstairs to join the children for recess. I haven't, to this day, been able to keep a straight face when something funny happens. The more I try to stifle a laugh, the worse I get, and I have no idea how to overcome this.

There were a few things not so funny, however. L.O. Donald had a new school building that fall. Not to be over-crowded, the principal decided to leave the third grade and two fourth grade classes in the old building. She didn't know me as well as some of the other teachers, but decided I would be in charge of the old building.

I had a little office above the book room. The principal decided that at the next PTA meeting, the fourth grade teachers were to stand before the parents and teachers and explain what they had taught in the first month of school. The teachers in the new building were called upon first. They proudly held up their new edition of the fourth grade reader and told how wonderful it was to have this new book.

When they got to me, I held up a ragged book and said, "I have done the best I could with what I have had, but by now, I'm sure that everyone knows that everything new stays in the new building, and everything old stays in the old building. And while I'm speaking, that also goes for the playground equipment."

I sat down. She was mad as hell at me and I knew it, the PTA knew it, and God knew it! But I didn't care, as we were all so tired of how we were treated in the old building.

She jumped up and said, "I have sent new books up there! And I was there yesterday and saw new bats and balls."

I said, "I checked the book room today, and there were no new books in there! And the balls and bats you saw came from my house! A friend and I went out and bought them with our money, so the kids in this building would have something new to start the new year. I have requested new books and new playground equipment and got neither."

That weekend, the PTA members tried to call me at home but I was not at home at the time. The lady I lived with said many calls had come from parents giving their support, saying if the principal didn't give me a good report at the end of the year, to let them know. I told her that I would fight my own battles. I knew she would not give me a good report, but the children in the old building did have new books for the rest of the year, so I was happy about that.

Now, all I had to do was to look up Dr. Walker one more time and ask him for another transfer. I would request a male principal. These old women tried to show that they had control over everyone and everything. That wasn't my method of handling people.

Children should be able to come to school with smiles on their faces—not be scared to death of the teachers and principal. Was it going to be left to me to write a new curriculum for the education classes of the future? I was no puppet and I wasn't going to hop up and down to a principal's antiquated way of thinking. I wasn't going to make children into puppets either. Teaching was a part of me, so I did it my way. I found that men principals figured you had gone to college and had about as much knowledge as they did, and they let me beat my own drums!

Instead of working for the city parks one summer, I decided to try something different. I loved dancing so much that I went downtown to the Fred Astaire Studio and told them that I would like to teach dancing. Each dance had 20 steps, and there were seven dances to learn: Fox Trot, Jitterbug, Waltz, Rumba, Tango, Samba, and Mambo. Had I gone down to sign up for a course, it would have cost $3,000.00 and many months to learn and perfect 140 steps. By training to be a teacher, it didn't cost me anything.

After learning only five steps of each dance, they had me teaching.

I learned fast! I knew for sure I was getting the power from Jesus again.

In most cases. a person could not have done all the things I did during a summer. I was not only giving lessons, but I was also doing some dancing on television with the Jerri Johnson Variety Show.

There was a joke in those days that getting a job on television was one that did not require years of experience, as television was only a few years old at the time. I loved the off-beat of the Mambo. The beating of the drums was hypnotic. I truly believed I was born to be a dancer.

One day, Fred Astaire, stopped by his studio in Dallas. The teachers told him about me and wanted to see us dance together. Meanwhile, I was just a block from the studio, but decided to walk around and "window shop" as it was a little early to go in. Mr. Astaire waited as long as he could, and said if he didn't leave, he'd miss his plane to New York. He hadn't been gone ten minutes when I walked in. I was excited but disappointed as they told me about my missed opportunity.

I would love to be able to say that I once danced with Fred Astaire! However, on second thought, I was frankly somewhat relieved. I had seen Fred Astaire and Ginger Rogers dance in all their movies. Had he danced with me, he would have probably laughed all the way to New York that day. Or he might have said, "You're no Ginger Rogers!" This way, he never knew what he missed (or didn't miss!).

That fall, my dance teacher transferred to the Frank DeVera Dance Studios. He wanted me to join him. I reminded him that I got my training at the Astaire Studio. But he reminded me that he was the one who trained me, and besides, I would get another $3,000 course free, so I went. Frank DeVera had three dance studios and was known as the best dancer in Dallas. He had a beautiful wife who had been his dance partner, but now she was taking time to start a family. He wanted me as his partner.

I would teach dancing in his studio at night, and on weekends we would dance at the hotels and country clubs in Dallas. We danced at the Baker Hotel for many months. The Aaron Brothers who owned the women's wholesale store were there every week to watch me dance.

Occasionally, we would dance for a Neiman-Marcus Style Show. Stanley Marcus bought a group course for his employees who wanted to come to the DeVera Studio once a week for a dance lesson. I received an extra bonus on that deal, which I used to buy a couple of extra beautiful exhibition dresses from Neiman-Marcus. A neighbor friend who worked at Neiman-Marcus, would call me when she saw something in stock that she thought I would like. Another favorite store sold used clothing from the rich and famous.

I bought some name brand clothing that looked like new, and they were the prettiest dresses I had ever owned. In fact, when I took my things to the cleaners, they would tell me I had the most beautiful wardrobe they had ever seen.

I don't know what made me so independent but I almost didn't get those two dresses from Neiman-Marcus. When Frank DeVera paid me the week before, he didn't include the commission for dancing at the style show. When I questioned him, he said that was a big one and he had talked them into the course while I was teaching school. I said, "But that wasn't our deal".

I walked out. The next night I didn't report to work. He had his secretary call me and I said that I keep my word and expect others to do the same, so I didn't feel like I wanted to work there. He got on the phone and said he had thought about it, and indeed, I should get half the commission on the class he had signed up, from the show we had done together. So I went back and we were always good friends after that and had many good times dancing together.

Once, while giving a dance lesson, I got so embarrassed and had to leave the dance room to laugh. Mr. DeVera and I would go out to the Country Clubs, and after the exhibition we would give out guest cards so the people could come in for a FREE dance lesson. If they wanted to continue, we had a Summer Special so they could take a small course for a big discount.

A man whom I had taught for an hour asked how he would be able to keep up with the lessons from the card. I was trying to explain to him that every time he came in for the next six times, we would punch a hole in his card.

But instead of saying his card, I said we would punch a hole in his hard.

I hurriedly said, "Mr. DeVera needs to come and explain it to you".

I rushed out of the room laughing. I ran into DeVera's office and told him that he needed to go in and close the deal. I got so tickled that I couldn't go back into the room. The guy signed up for the summer special and became a good dancer, and signed up for the big course. He helped me teach a few classes at a country club, and was kind enough never to mention my embarrassing moment.

This is funny! One of my friends was trying to teach her student how to waltz, while the rest of us were observing. She was trying to have him come up on the balls of his feet.

She kept saying, "Dance on your balls–dance on your balls!"

We all started laughing and her student finally said, "Wouldn't that be a bit painful?" (She ran out of the room—but later married the guy.)

While I was working at night I encountered an experience that caused me to start thinking about buying a car. When I finished my lesson at 10:00 o'clock, I would go home on the streetcar. One night, a weird-acting guy got off the streetcar when I did. He started chasing me, but I outran him. I was living with a lady and her daughter, and they heard me running and had the door open. The next night, I asked to leave work early so I could get off at the local drug store while it was still open. When I saw that he also got off, I called the police and the policeman took me home. The policeman happened to be the dad of one of my fourth grade pupils. The entire class knew what had happened by the time I got to school the next morning.

In those days, we started each day with a prayer. It started out with, "For the night of calm and quiet, for the rest and refreshment received, I thank Thee, Good Lord. (By now the children were laughing) Whether we sleep, or whether we wake, Thou art not far from us, but ever present as our gracious Father. Thy hand we take as we go forth this morning, knowing that Thou will give strength for every task, wisdom for every problem, and help in time of need. Shield us from every assault of the evil one, and guide us in the way of truth and light. Amen."

We all laughed and a little boy brought me a switch blade knife. He said he had two, so he thought I should have one of them.

I said, "I thank you, and I feel sure that the good Lord who watches over me, thanks you, also!"

The next night, DeVera walked behind me to the street car and the same weird guy was there looking at me. I went to the end of the line, and when he got on the street car, DeVera said, "Okay, I'm taking you home."

It was at this time that Ann Priest became a co-owner of the DeVera Dance Studios. She suggested that I move in with her and her daughter, India Ann, whom she called Punkin. I wouldn't have to travel at night, and it turned out to be the best decision of my life, as the three of us had some wonderful times together during the next few years. I drove to school with some teachers until I had the time to buy a car. Ann, Punkin, and I triple-dated and traveled together. These were the most fun days of my life!

I started attending the Episcopal Church with Ann and Punkin. To my surprise, my dance partner, Frank DeVera and his wife went to the same church. I took some lessons and decided to join the church. The priest asked Ann and me if we would teach Sunday School. With both of us teaching together, one of us could still go out of town when we wanted to. Or if we both left, we could get a substitute. What we didn't know was that we were required to go to meetings on Tuesday nights to prepare ourselves for teaching on Sunday.

After about three years, I told the priest that after teaching school all day, teaching dancing at night, and teaching Sunday School on Sundays, I was beginning to feel like the postman who takes a walk on his day off. He agreed that everyone needs to take a break once in a while. We talked about other ways of using our talents, and I ended up giving him some dance lessons (at no cost). He came to my house for lessons.

When he gave the teachers a party at the end of the school year, he surprised them by having us entertain them with a samba. Everyone was having a glass of champagne, and enjoyed seeing their priest, Father Cragon, dance. Then we did a jitterbug, and that got everyone up on the dance floor.

It was soon time to leave for the summer and we celebrated the end of his dance classes by going to the Statler Hotel. This gave him a chance to show off the dance steps he had learned. Carol Channing was entertaining that night.

We went up to her and said, "Hello Dolly, we enjoyed your show."

She told us she bet we didn't enjoy it as much as she enjoyed watching us dance.

Dallas entertainers would often meet in an "after hour" club in an old building upstairs near downtown Dallas. Most people went there to relax, drink beer, smoke cigarettes, chat, and listen to music. I found it interesting to meet people in show business. Most were the musicians who enjoyed having a jam session with other musicians. Sometimes, it seemed as though life was a never-ending party. However, I didn't do this often because I always went to church on Sundays no matter what time I got home on Saturday night.

Now, I enjoy watching people of fame on television, especially someone with musical or acting talent. I often wonder what they must have sacrificed to succeed. I admire them so much, even though I was not willing to make the sacrifices myself to become famous. I thought I had to do everything "my way". "Fame" was not on my priority list. However, I did believe in living to the fullest.

I could have danced all night

Ronnie Shipman and Norene

I step to a different drum beat

When I was invited by the Dallas
Chamber of Commerce, I thought
I was a guest–not a guest speaker!
Lord, keep me from laughing!

An Enchanted Evening

VACATION IN CALIFORNIA

BALBOA BEACH

Norene, India Ann,
and Annabelle

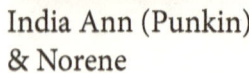

India Ann (Punkin)
& Norene

Chapter 6

I Did it My Way - Finally!

Summer arrived and Ann and I took off for California in my new 1955 pink Chevy. Punkin stayed with her dad, who was divorced from Ann. Punkin wanted to stay in Dallas to be with her friends; but later flew out to be with us. Ann had lived in California and knew many interesting people (like John Wayne). When we went to church in Los Angeles, Robert Young, the TV star of "Father Knows Best" ushered us to our seats. He asked us where we would like to sit and we said, "Father knows best!" We were thrilled to see movie stars out there in California.

To keep from getting rusty, I decided to take some dance lessons from a very famous dancer named Ramon Talavera. He wanted me to become his dance partner, but my heart was in Dallas, so I went home at the end of the summer. Marlon Brando took bongo drum lessons from Ramon. I took a couple of bongo drum lessons also, but spent most of my time dancing. When Walt Disney wanted one or two of his characters to do a little dance, he would take a few lessons from Ramon. He was also the host of the dance convention in California that summer.

Meanwhile, I had transferred to another school in Dallas called James Bowie Elementary. The principal's name was Mr. Anderson. He asked if I would enjoy teaching health and science. I told him that health was always my favorite subject, but science was my worst!

I liked challenges and I liked meeting new people, so I told him I thought I could make him proud and do a pretty good job. I taught health and science in the fourth through eighth grades. For Halloween, I hung a large skeleton by my door, and it later became a part of my teaching. I printed the names of all the bones on it, and was able to teach the names of all of them to the children. I had learned the names from a human physiology class I had taken in college. I didn't rush it. I would teach the arm bones one week and the leg bones another week for the first five minutes after they came into the room. In science lessons, the children loved doing the experiments from the science kits.

They also enjoyed collecting critters. Once, we had a lizard in the room and one of the children said, "Teacher, winter is coming and we need to let our lizard go so it can hibernate". Another child argued that we should keep it because it had become our friend, and besides, it was too late to find another lizard! One child wondered why it needed another lizard. A boy yelled out, "Good gosh, Johnny, don't you know nothin'?"

Sometimes by staying quiet, I found that the children would help one another with their studies. Another day, I thought I had a beautiful lesson prepared, but as I was beginning to talk, I noticed that not one child was looking at me. So I followed their eyes. The kids had been to the turtle races at Fair Park and they got to keep the turtles. They were painted blue, red, green, and yellow. The children had lined them up while I was checking the roll. They were having their own turtle race, so I just sat down and enjoyed the race with them. Then they told me and the class everything they had learned about turtles. Some came with encyclopedias the following day.

One thing led to another, and soon they were learning to teach to their classmates.

One day, as I opened my desk drawer to get a pen to check the roll, there was a tiny grass snake in my drawer. I thought I was going to jump out of my skin! The children thought it was funny, but I quickly supplied the snake with a container. I told the children to add a few rocks, grass, and some water to the container.

Soon there were other snakes added to the collection. With the help of encyclopedias and library books, the children soon learned about many different kinds of snakes. Someone either let them out, or they found the way out all by themselves, but word got around the school that there were snakes crawling around in the basement. The rest rooms were in the basement, so the little children were half-scared to go to the rest room. We finally opened the doors, and hopefully they all found their way outside. I was pleased never to see them again.

The children also collected butterflies and put them in a jar with a cotton ball of ammonia or something that killed them. They then displayed them on the bulletin board. One boy failed to do this and pinned his butterfly on the bulletin board with its wings still flapping! This was one crazy class, but they learned many things about nature.

I never knew what to expect when I arrived in the classroom each day.

My best friend at this school was Marcile Clifton. I believe she was the funniest person I had ever met. She liked getting a party going with a few of her friends. She was the secretary of the James Bowie Elementary School and her long time friend, Nell, was the nurse. They had a friend who was a first grade teacher who seemed very quiet at school, but was everything but quiet after 4:00 o'clock. Those gals had been on many fishing trips together and decided to take me on a long weekend with them. We had to go home on a Thursday afternoon and call in "sick" for the following day (Friday). We would have a long weekend to fish and have fun.

When they came to pick me up, I said, "I hear you've all got the three-day measles. I don't know whether I want to go with you sick gals! I might catch something!"

Marcile said, "Get your butt in the car! We don't have anything that a good stiff drink won't cure!"

So off we went to Lake Texoma in hopes of catching a bunch of fish. She not only knew how to fish, but she really knew how to cook them. I saw that she and Nell also knew how to get a boat in and out of the water faster than most men would do it.

On Saturday afternoon, the clouds gathered, and we got news on the radio that a tornado was headed for Lake Texoma. I jumped out of the boat too soon, and waded out in mud up to my hips. The others told me to go on to the cabin and get a shower while they pulled the boat out of the water and hitched it back to the car. They were getting nervous because they knew their husbands would be worrying about them. I decided to brighten their mood. When they came to the cabin, I had some soft music playing and was doing a sort of ballet around the room in my shorty nightgown.

Marcile walked in and said "Stop dancing, Ding-Bat, and get some blue jeans on. We are about to be blown to bits!"

I told her that if we were going to heaven, I would look more angelic in my nightgown. She fixed us all a drink and said that maybe that would calm our nerves. I think she put a double shot in her glass. I told her to calm down or she wouldn't know whether she was "washing or hanging it out". Once the storm passed (not hitting us directly), she was able to get in touch with her husband, Horace, and she calmed down. She started cooking and we had a great time. I was just a social drinker. One drink to be sociable would last me all night, because I didn't like the taste of mixed drinks.

The following Monday, I met my principal in the hall between classes. Unbeknownst to me, he had already talked to Marcile and Nell, and had already figured out that we had all skipped school together.

He said, "I was surprised when you were out Friday. I have never seen you sick."

I could never lie, so in my nervous state, I started laughing. I said, "Marcile and Nell said they thought I was getting the three-day measles." (Holding my arms up for him to see)

He took my arms in his hands and examined them carefully, then said, "Looks more like mosquito bites to me!"

Thank goodness, the bell rang, and I hurriedly went back to my room. When I saw Marcile, she was laughing, and I said, "Marcile, you're going to get me fired!"

But she and Mr. Anderson were good friends, and she said he wouldn't report us to the main office, so long as we didn't go fishing every Friday.

I had a saying, "I'm not wild, it's my friends who always get me in trouble."

I liked Mr. Anderson. He had been a coach before he became a principal. He always looked strong, and tall, and he had a suntan even during the winter months. However, I never felt completely at ease with someone who was my boss. One day, he asked how I was going to spend the weekend. I told him I had a date with a doctor, and had invited him to my place for a steak dinner.

I was apprehensive as to how it would turn out as I seldom cooked for my dates.

I said, "What was I thinking? With my luck, the steaks will probably turn out to be dry and tough!"

He said, "Let me give you my expertise on cooking steaks, and you won't go wrong. Buy some nice thick T-Bones with some marbling in them."

I said, "Marbling?"

He said, "Yes, that small white fat makes the steaks juicy and tender. About an hour before cooking, put the steaks on a platter, and put some olive oil on each side. Add a little lemon juice or a spoonful of wine. Grind coarse peppercorns over them and press it into the steaks on both sides. Add a little salt and they are ready to be cooked."

On Monday, he sat by me during lunch and asked how my dinner party turned out. I told him that I was tempted to call him to come over and cook them for me, but I did everything like he suggested, and they were delicious.

I added a tossed salad, a baked potato, and a glass of wine. Ummmm! Good!

Mr. Anderson moved to another state that summer, because his wife's health was failing and she needed to live in a more favorable dry climate.

Fortunately, I got another man for a principal. His name was Mr. Morrill. He told me that the school would have a new gym in the fall and wondered if I would like to be the new physical education teacher. I jumped at the chance! I couldn't believe I was going to be paid to teach children to play games and to be connected with the physical education department. My boss was the same person who was in charge of the summer activities on the playgrounds and city parks. I found that he had highly recommended me to the principal, and that made me feel good.

Being the physical education teacher was perhaps the reason the principal assigned me to be in charge of the Safety Patrol at our school. The seventh and eight grade boys volunteered to be on patrol duty. Half of them would take the morning shift and the other half would take the afternoon shift. Come rain or shine, they were on their designated corners in their yellow jackets with their stop signs.

Their "gear" was kept in the lockers in the old P.E. room in the basement. I had meetings one afternoon each week to organize those on patrol duty.

We would go over things like the importance of promptness in getting to the corner on time, what to do in case of their absence from school, how to stop cars, and how to help the children cross the street. I also talked with each class once a week as they came to the gym, to make them aware of following the rules. I stressed that they must go to the corners every time to cross the street and never to jay-walk in the middle of the block.

I was going from my school one Friday to Arlington to spend the night with my sister, when suddenly, I got stopped by a policeman. I believe I was going 30 miles an hour in a 20 mile an hour school zone. The policeman recognized me and reminded me that he was the one who took me home eight years earlier when a man followed me home several nights after I got off the streetcar. We had a good visit and he told me his daughter, who was my pupil back then, was currently in her first year of college. I didn't get a ticket, but it gave me something to think about. The children were already gone but we were still in a school zone.

I told my patrol the following week, that besides getting the children across the street, not to be afraid to use the whistle if the cars were not slowing down while the children were still on the corners of the school ground. I continued the safety meetings with the classes each week.

Then a very bad accident happened early one morning. A child got hit by a car. I ran to the office to find out the details. The principal told me that a boy was killed. I went into the rest room and started crying. When I finally came out, the principal told me that he was very proud of me and the patrol boys, and that this was in no way a reflection on us. He said that the boy had transferred to our school the day before. He had not had time to learn the rules of correct street crossing. His dad had dropped him off early that morning on his way to work. The boy jumped out of the car, ran behind his dad's car and right into the path of an oncoming car. It was too early for the patrols to be on the corners. The driver simply didn't see the boy in time, and the boy died before the ambulance arrived. I didn't say anything to the patrol boys because they had done everything I trained them to do. But I learned that we can sometimes work so hard to perfect our jobs and to protect the children, and bad things can still happen.

On cold mornings, I would open the gym for the children and we would have "sockhops". Most of the children already knew how to jitterbug, boogie woogie, and bop. It didn't take long for those who knew, to teach those who didn't know, because a blow of the whistle would mean to quickly change partners. We all loved Little Richard, Jerry Lee Lewis, Elvis, and other popular performers. Even the teachers would occasionally stick their heads in to see what was going on.

I later entered the fourth through eighth grades in a city-wide square dancing festival. My boss in the P.E. department told me that my students were by far, the best dancers there. I showed them how to keep their knees bent slightly, so they could move smoothly— instead of bouncing when they would promenade home.

I also did many PTA programs, such as the big Christmas program. I had taught eight dances -- one being the "Dance of the Dolls". Even Mr. and Mrs. Santa danced. Another program I did was a Stephen Foster musical called "Way Down South". The children did many songs and dances. The Dallas Times Herald staff came out and took pictures and did a write-up on it for the morning paper. I was surprised as I had no idea who called them to come out to the school.

The children always remembered their programs, and told me that I was different from any teacher they ever had. That was the nicest compliment I could receive, and anyone who took one look at some of the little old lady teachers who seemed to have forgotten how to smile, would agree.

At one of the PTA programs, Mr. DeVera came out and we did an exhibition at the end of the program. Word got to the community that we were going to dance, and there was standing room only that night. Many were standing out in the hall, as well as at the back of the auditorium.

I loved my teaching job so much, and I loved the dancing job just as much, if not more. If you really want something, you must really go for it—otherwise, there will always be a missing link in your life.

At one of the dance exhibitions in Dallas, I met a good looking doctor, Bob Speegle. He was building a hospital in Garland. He came to the dance studio for some lessons, but was already a terrific dancer. After his lesson, we would go out at 10:00 o'clock and jitterbug for a couple of hours. My tonsils had been giving me problems, so instead of taking me home one night, he dropped me off at his clinic and said he would see me the next morning for the operation to remove my tonsils. Sure enough, he was there bright and early. As he put me under, he put the contraption over my nose and mouth and sang, "And all the monkeys aren't in a zoo-zoo-zoo."

When I awakened it was all over and my friend, Marcile, came to pick me up to take me home that afternoon. Dr. Speegle and I had many good times together, but he was very busy getting his hospital completed and his business started. I was busy working day and night. He later married his sister's best friend while I was chasing around one summer in California.

I was once told by a friend that I was the only gal she knew that she could trust with her husband. I jokingly said, "Wow! That's either the highest compliment or the biggest insult that I've ever received."

For a short time, my dance partner, Frank DeVera, booked us at a little club on Oak Lawn in Dallas. It was owned by Jack Ruby, who also owned a strip club downtown. I felt a little uneasy dancing there because Mr. Ruby seemed weird, like he belonged with the Mafia. A great Mexican band was performing there, so we went ahead and danced there for a while. One night, the stripper, Candy Barr, came there to watch me dance.

She followed me into the rest room and said, "I'd give anything if I could dance like you."

I said, "Honey, you don't need to worry about fancy footwork, because believe me, no one is looking at your feet!"

Mr. Ruby wanted to get a show together and take us to a club in Oklahoma for the weekend, but I told DeVera that I was not going to be in the same show as a stripper. I told him it would be all over the Dallas Schools by Monday morning. So far, I had a fairly good reputation, and I didn't want to spoil it over one show. While I didn't ever think I was better than anyone else, I did have a set of values through which to filter all my decisions. In fact, I talked DeVera into doing our shows in a better class of clubs. We started dancing at the best country clubs and hotels in Dallas.

I am sure by now you recognize the name, Jack Ruby. He was the man who shot and killed Lee Harvey Oswald, who had killed President Kennedy. (That happened several years after our association with him, but I recognized him as soon as I tuned in on the TV news that fateful day.) They mentioned that he always had policemen around him, and I remembered when we were in his club, there were always policemen there. I wondered at the time if they were keeping an eye on Ruby or if it was just a place where they could hang out. Ruby later died of cancer while in prison.

Someone once said to me that I was the most famous dancer in Dallas. But I remarked that, Frank DeVera is the most famous dancer and he had three dance studios to prove it. So then she said that I was the most famous woman dancer.

I said, "Wrong again! More than three-fourths of the people in Dallas have probably heard of Candy Barr, but I doubt that many people in Dallas have ever heard of me."

I just danced because I enjoyed it. I didn't care about fame. I certainly wouldn't have traded places with Candy Barr. In 1957, she had to spend some time in prison for possession of marijuana. On December 30, 2005, she died at age 70.

A booking agent told me he could get my name in lights in Las Vegas. As I looked at the lights, I knew that was not what I wanted out of life. I would have had to give up teaching, living in Texas, and would have had my hours so booked, that I wouldn't have been able to do what I wanted to do.

Right then, I was in control of my life. If I wanted a weekend free to go out of town, I just didn't book myself to work. Teaching was my livelihood, so I felt obligated there, but dancing was my hobby, so I could feel free to control my hours as I wished. Everyone has hobbies and I always chose those where I could make money to pay for my hobby.

Once, after an exhibition, I was going around to all the tables and handing out guest cards to the patrons for a free dance lesson. I would get an extra commission on everyone who signed up for a dance course. Two doctor's sat at one of the tables. They asked me what I had on my skin, as my skin had a pretty glow under the bright lights. I jokingly told them that it was my own secret concoction, and went on to the next table.

The following day, the same doctor's came to my apartment and said they were willing to pay me for my "secret concoction".

Finally, I said, "You can have it "free". I was too embarrassed to tell them the night before that it was just baby oil!

One night when I was doing an exhibition in Dallas with Frank DeVera, we met a guy who was a member of the Dallas School Board. I already knew I couldn't hide in Dallas, so we all had a good time dancing. As I left, I jokingly told him that I wouldn't tell anyone I met him on a dance floor if he wouldn't tell anyone where he met me. We had a big laugh. Those were the days when many teachers lived like they had one foot in the grave, while I lived like there was no tomorrow.

Another time, I went to a little club that had a Mexican band. We danced on a slab outside, and I was having the time of my life jitterbugging. Suddenly, I heard a voice on the loud speaker say, "Is there anyone who hasn't noticed this lovely lady dancing? Let's give a big applause to Miss Nygaard, my health and science teacher in the seventh and eight grade."

I couldn't believe it! I was so surprised and pleased to see my pupil with his own band.

On several occasions, on behalf of the physical education department, I always felt honored when I was asked to serve as a hostess to greet attendees at different school meetings and also at a convention at a hotel in downtown Dallas.

On one occasion, my principal told me that the Jaycees (Dallas Junior Chamber of Commerce) would like for me to greet people at the Statler Hotel as they arrived, and to direct them to the special exhibit called "Dallas on Parade" that was described in the pamphlet I handed to each person. It explained that "Dallas on Parade" was a model used to describe the story of Dallas and to educate the public as to what the community offered to the nation. The Jaycees were made up of progressive and aggressive business leaders in the city of Dallas.

At one point, I was asked to begin to direct people to the auditorium to begin the program. As I picked up a copy of the program, I noticed my name on it.

I remarked to one of the Jaycees ,"I thought I was a guest, not a guest speaker! What am I supposed to speak about?"

He said, "Read the first sentence on the pamphlet you handed out and do the best you can."

The first sentence on the pamphlet stated that "Dallas on Parade" is to educate people of the city of Dallas how we work, how we play, how we worship, to let people know of our business, social, and religious life." Wow!

I had about two minutes to figure out what to tell - and what would be best left untold. As I went up to the podium, I jokingly let them know that someone forgot to tell me that I was supposed to be a speaker. I managed in a few minutes to tell them how I contributed my work, social, and religious life to the city of Dallas.

I wanted to laugh, because at the same time I was thinking about the things I should probably leave out. I explained how I would teach school in the daytime, teach dancing at night, do exhibitions on weekends, and teach Sunday School and go to church services on Sundays. People would say, "You must like teaching to do it day and night."

I always thought of life as an adventure. In my spare time, I read many books. Most were on self-improvement of the body, mind, and spirit. I was interested in metaphysics, fasting, and health. I also signed up for courses on various health topics - health clubs, spas, massages, yoga, golf, tennis, hypnosis, positive thinking lectures, and Bible classes. I would also fast at least one week every year, usually in the spring. This felt invigorating to my body, soothing to my nerves, and kept my mind focused in a positive direction.

I can relate to a remark I once heard, "If you enjoy what you're doing, you never work a day of your life."

Did I say I was just a social drinker?
I meant to say, SOCIABLE

I'm not so bad, Lord.
It's my friends who
get me in trouble!

Ann and Norene—took the
Champagne flight to Las Vegas.

VACATION IN MEXICO

George's little sailfish–73 lbs.

Norene's sailfish–110 lbs.

Garden of Eden

Mexican Poppies

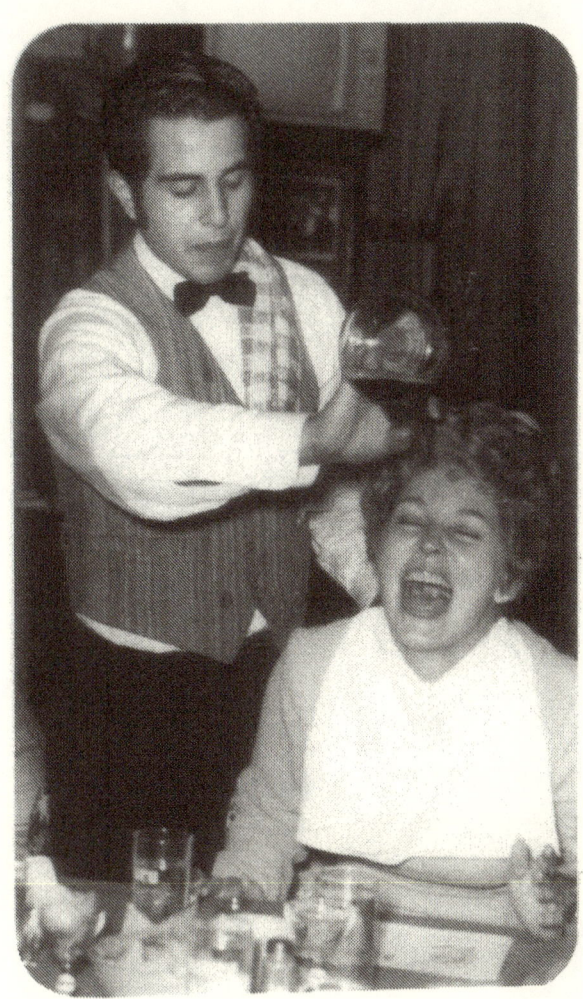

Wow! this is good!
You say it's a juice
that makes me happy?

Born to be wild!

Sorry Charles—I meant to say,
I'll punch a hole in your CARD.

Chapter 7

A Little on the Wild Side

I learned early in life to "fake it til I make it". Not to be deceiving, but I found that if you act with confidence, people will have confidence in you. Then eventually, you just might have confidence in yourself. When I applied for a job, instead of thinking I might not be able to handle it, I went in with a smile on my face and an attitude that this could be the adventure of a lifetime! Losing was not a word in my vocabulary. I was never turned down for a job, nor was I ever fired. Lord only knows, there were many times I could have been asked, "What were you thinking?"

Once I flew to California for the weekend, and my friends took me to a little club to eat and dance before I was to leave to come back home. I missed my plane, so we hung out a few more hours until the next plane left. I got back to my job in Dallas just as the bell rang. The teachers and principal were standing on the front porch having bets on whether I would make it back on time. As my foot touched the school ground, the bell rang, and I said, "How's that for timing it?"

Another time, a teacher friend and I drove to Texarkana, which was over 100 miles from Dallas, to join her friends for a party. On the way back, we stopped in McKinney for breakfast. Then we drove to Dallas and up to the school just as the bell rang, and together we said, "How's that for timing it?" We were both fourth grade teachers at that school.

I had one principal who was a stickler for the faculty to arrive promptly for meetings on Wednesday mornings at 7:30. One morning, I walked in holding a speeding ticket, and all I could say was, "At least, I tried!" Even the principal laughed at my misfortune.

Once my friend, Ann told me she had received a call from friends in El Paso, suggesting we meet them and they would take us over the border to Mexico.

I said, "But Ann, I just had a boating accident and I am wearing a brace around my waist, so I am in dire pain!"

She convinced me that by the time I drink a margarita, I will feel no pain. So we caught the next plane to El Paso.

Sure enough, after one drink, I was clapping my hands to the Mexican music, and making those funny rolling mouth sounds that ended with ah, ah, ah, ah, ah. Ann told them that I could dance better than their Mexican gals. With that, they jerked the table cloth off the table and the band played a fast tune. Everyone was yelling ah, ah, ah, ah, ah. She then told them that I was dancing with a brace on, and the Mexicans clapped as I got off the table.

I later thought that if someone started dancing on the table in Texas, they would probably be locked up. But I believed in having a good time and entertaining others. I didn't get obnoxious or drink too much. Just good, lively music would lift my spirits. I can relate to a song I recently heard, "I was somewhere between raisin'hell and amazin' grace."

Another time, Ann and I caught the Champagne Flight out of Los Angeles to Las Vegas for the weekend. As we were playing the slot machines, I heard a band start playing, "When the Saints Go Marching In".

I said, "Ann, that sounds exactly like the band 'Cell Block Seven' from Dallas."

We looked up from the slot machines and they marched right by us and recognized us. It was fun to meet someone we knew. They had drinks sent over to us.

That night we met Micky Rooney. He was losing around $20,000 at the table. I asked him the date of his birth, then told him what his lucky number was. Then Ann and I decided we needed to get some rest. Mickey came out about $20,000 ahead, and he sent the bell captain to our door to find out what cut I wanted from his earnings. I told him that I don't accept money from men, but if he had a picture, I would accept that. After a few minutes, the guy knocked on our door again and handed me a large picture of Mickey Rooney. He had written at the bottom, "To my friend, Norene, from Mickey Rooney." I still have that picture, as well as the memory of the good time we had that weekend in Las Vegas.

Ann and I went up and down the strip seeing all the shows. I enjoyed the Sammy Davis show so much, I went twice. Sammy had so much talent in his singing and dancing, and I was so intrigued. What a showman he was!

Some people ask me if I was wild, and I ask them what they consider wild. I loved music, I loved having a good time with friends, but I was brought up to be a lady. In my wildest dreams, I wouldn't act like some gals I've seen on TV pulling up their blouses like they do in New Orleans to get beads, or like the repulsive behavior shown on the Jerry Springer show. There is a big difference between fun and vulgarity! As much as I like jokes, when I tell one, I prefer leaving something to the imagination. I don't have to use a vulgar word to make it funny. I do have a sense of humor - we all need to laugh to stay well.

I liked all kinds of music, not just popular and Mexican music. There was a small club in Dallas where there was a piano player who really knew how to play to a crowd. I don't remember her name, but she was a heavy-set black woman and she played and sang jazz, blues, or whatever was requested.

Her opening song was always, "A Good Man is Hard to Find". By the time everyone had a drink or two, she was singing it a little differently, "A Hard Man is Good to Find!" She was something else! She kept us laughing all night long.

Ann knew many wealthy men, and she used to say, "Stick with me and you'll wear diamonds." I'd tell her that I heard diamond rings cut off circulation! I was single and liked to mingle! However, she did introduce me to a real nice Texas gentleman, George McGee, who had been a lawyer in Kilgore , Texas.

He lived in California, and we went to interesting places that I had never been before. He was fun to be with. I had never eaten lobster until I went to California, and he showed me how to crack it open and dip it in all that good, spiced, melted butter. He was retired and lived off the revenue of some old oil wells in Texas. His best buddy was Robert Mitchem, whom I was thrilled to meet along with a few other movie stars. Several times we went to the Mitchem's home to swim.

The following Christmas, the Mitchem's invited us to Acapulco, Mexico to spend the holidays, and watch him make the movie, "Bandito". One day, we went deep-sea fishing. The hotel where I stayed recorded the weight of everyone's fish on a chart in the lobby, and offered an extra week's stay to the one who had caught the biggest sailfish by the end of the week. I was ahead until the last day–my fish was 110 pounds, but someone caught one that weighed in at 114 pounds. I couldn't have stayed anyway, because it was time to get back to school after the holidays. There were pictures made of me bringing in the sailfish and of it leaping high in the air.

I went back to Dallas with a good suntan, because I spent every day on the beach. One of the beach bums was a donkey. People would put a bottle of beer in the donkey's mouth, and he would turn it up and drink it in about three gulps. I had pictures made of me sitting on that little donkey who was always on the beach all day.

At night we went dancing. While George McGee (Mitchem's friend), didn't come to dance, he enjoyed watching me dance. He didn't mind tipping the gigolo's to dance with me when they came to our table.

One thing I liked about being around Mitchem and McGee was that they were full of jokes. They told me that I reminded them of a lady centipede, who crossed her thousand legs, and said, "No, No, A thousand times, No!"

Through Robert Mitchem and George McGee, I also had the pleasure of meeting Marilyn Monroe, and we all had a good time in Dallas. She had been to Acapulco, Mexico and was at the Baker Hotel. Mitchem and McGee had stopped in Dallas to see me, but were on their way to New Orleans to go fishing and partying. Mitchem and

Monroe had made a movie together, and they were all friends. We had dinner and a visit at a famous steakhouse downtown. I had to remind myself that I had to teach school the next day, so I went on home, after wishing them a good time in New Orleans.

In 1955, I bought my first new car. It was a shocking pink Chevrolet. I loved it! I also bought a three-piece set of shocking pink luggage. So whether I was at an airport, or driving around Dallas, you can be sure I was spotted wherever I went!

One weekend, I went to see Mother in Cranfills Gap, and on my way back to Dallas, I heard all this honking, and a driver making motions to pull over. He was a lawyer friend, and we chatted a while. He asked me what I was doing 50 miles out of Dallas and I told him I had gone home for Mother's Day.

He said, "Speaking of Mother's Day, you won't believe what ours was like. There were about twenty people there and my mother started yelling that she had lost her teeth and no one could eat until we had found them. Everyone looked in her bed, under the bed, in the bathroom, and everywhere we could imagine. Finally after about thirty minutes, someone yelled 'they're in your mouth!' Then she said, 'I know! This is Mother's Day and everyone is so busy talking to each other, that this is the only way I figured any of you are going to notice me. It's my day, - Hello'. " He told me a couple of jokes and we headed back to Dallas.

The lawyer was a friend of my friend, George McGee, who lived in California. That fall, when deer season opened, he invited George and me to his place to taste his cooking. He had made a big pot of deer stew. He had cooked it with wine, and it was a gourmet's delight. The two had been friends since their younger days in Kilgore and they kept me laughing at some of their experiences together as young lawyers. I could clearly see why the three of us became such good friends. We were three of a kind!

As I mentioned before, Las Vegas had become one of my favorite places to go to have a good time. There were many shows to see. The rooms, food, and drinks were very reasonable, so it didn't cost much to have a good time. My twin brother, Noran, had become a traveling man, and as he came through Dallas, it didn't take much persuasion to wonder if I wanted to ride with him to Las Vegas. He had built some roads and highways in the area, so he knew many people and some of the best places to go. It didn't take me long to pack, and we were on our way, chanting, "Las Vegas , Here We Come!"

When we arrived, we went to pick up tickets to the Red Skelton show, and found they were sold out. So we decided to go next door to eat. To our surprise, there was Red Skelton, eating with three other people. I suggested we see if our waiter would do us a favor for five bucks. We could ask him if he would go to Skelton's table and tell him that we had driven there from Dallas to see his show, but were unable to get tickets. Then tell him we have listened to him for years on the radio and are thrilled at least to see him in person. Noran agreed, so I started looking to see which one was our waiter, as they were all black.

Noran said, "Wasn't it that guy across from us? You're supposed to notice all the guys, I just look at the cute gals."

I said, "I don't know, they all look alike to me".

Finally, our waiter delivered our message. Red Skelton stood up, looked at us, did his little finger wave, sent us two guest tickets, and walked out. We were thrilled! We figured if they were sold out, we would either get a back seat or have to stand up at the back. To our surprise, we were ushered to the front seat.

As he came out on stage, he looked at us, did his little finger wave, and the show began. Red Skelton introduced his band leader, Count Basie.

Count Basie said, "Thank you, Bob Hope!"

Red said, "But I'm not Bob Hope –- I'm Red Skeleton!"

Count Basie said, "Oh, I'm sorry. I can't tell you white boys apart!"

We did a little gambling with the nickel and dime machines and headed out for California the next day. I stopped to visit with friends and Noran headed up toward the Washington area.

A few years later, I saw Red Skelton coming into Palm Springs as I was leaving. I waved at him, and he waved back.

My other hero in the entertainment business was Bob Hope. I admired him because he gave up his Christmas vacation every year to entertain the servicemen overseas. We were all very patriotic in those days, and he gave so much of himself with all the trips he made. Some of them were quite dangerous, but he and his group managed to come through all of them safely, and a good time was had by all. We always looked forward to seeing his Christmas shows on television.

I went to see Bob Hope in Dallas at Fair Park, and it was a thrill to see him in person.

He said, "These jet planes can really get you where you want to go in a hurry. For instance, when we left Los Angeles, we had two rabbits in the plane with us, and when we arrived in Dallas , we still had just two rabbits!"

I seldom missed the opportunity to see and hear the famous and interesting people who came to Dallas. I went to Fair Park to see Billy Graham, the famous evangelist, who had become the rage all over the country with his dynamic sermons that drew crowds like we had never before seen. I also went to see Norman Vincent Peale one weekend at SMU. I had read and enjoyed many of his books. (I read "The Power of Positive Thinking" three times.)

I was also intrigued by a lecture given by the men who had explored King Tut's Tomb. About a dozen men had gone in there, but most had died from the gases that had formed within the tomb. As I remember, only three of them survived.

Of course, when Sally Rand appeared at the State Fair one year, I got a front seat to see if she really could keep one of the fans in front of her at all times, as she danced (almost nude). She could.

One very special weekend, I went to the Fair Park Auditorium in Dallas to see Dean Martin and Jerry Lewis. They were terrific. Jerry was so funny and Dean had a singing style one would never forget. They seemed to have a good time entertaining everyone. I can still hear Dean singing, "Everybody loves somebody some time."

I enjoyed doing things spontaneously. Once, I flew to Florida with some friends. I had never experienced turbulence, and we hit some air pockets.

I had no idea what was happening to us. I thought it was over, and headed for the rest room, only to have the turbulence start up again, and had to stay in there for a while. When I returned, I showed my friends that my plastic and metal bag, which was shaped like a lunch basket, had fallen and was broken.

I looked across the aisle, and saw a baby who was sleeping very calmly. I asked the mother, "Does your baby have some kind of tranquilizer in his milk?"

I stayed at the New Cadillac hotel in Miami, and they were having a Cha-Cha-Cha dance contest in the dining room. I was asked to enter, and I won the first place trophy. It was much like DeVera and I did at hotels in Dallas. Several people were picked to dance, and the winner was determined by popular applause. The only difference was that we gave the winner a bottle of Champagne and a ticket for a free dance lesson to be given at DeVera's studio.

The next day, we decided to fly to Cuba since we were so close. As we arrived, the cab driver warned us to lay low, because someone had tried to kill Bastista and the police were everywhere. Needless to say, I didn't leave the hotel and I was glad to get out of there the following day. This was just before Fidel Castro took over the ruling of Cuba.

Another time, I flew with a friend to Houston. We met another couple whom we knew who had invited us to join them. We drove together to Galveston. On the flight, we flew into the worst electrical storm we had ever encountered. By the time we got off the plane, we were wringing wet with perspiration. But since it was raining outside, no one noticed our appearance.

The men were both lawyers, and had plenty of money to gamble. I really didn't know how to gamble, so I preferred to go to the ballroom and listen to the music. People had been getting by with gambling in Galveston because it was being done on boats or barges off-shore, or at the Flagship Hotel, which is the only hotel in North America built over water.

Word on the street was that this was the last weekend to gamble in Texas, because the officials were planning to dump the slot machines into the ocean after that weekend. I can't verify if it went that far, but I do believe the gambling was stopped. I didn't want to gamble because I figured it was against the law, or they wouldn't be trying to stop it.

As I walked into the ballroom, the band members recognized me and started playing my favorite song, "Mona Lisa". They used to play that same song when I walked into the ballroom at the Baker

Hotel where I danced many times. I was surprised to see them in Galveston, but enjoyed listening to the music. It had stopped raining by the time we got back to Houston, and we boarded a plane and arrived in Dallas a short time later.

Music was a very important part of my life. It was in my bones! I will always remember the first time I heard the song, "When I Fall In Love".

I didn't know who Johnny Mathis was at the time, but he had a voice like I had never heard. I was on my way to school, and I pulled over to the side of the road to write it down so I could buy the record. Soon after, I heard his song, "Danger, Heartbreak Ahead". Little did I know, how much this song would affect me in the days ahead.

I had gone out with a good looking guy from "Old Miss". He had his own business and a new car. It was the first of its kind, a Thunderbird. I won't give his name since he turned out to be THE DATE FROM HELL! I told him that Johnny Mathis would be in Dallas the following weekend. We agreed it would be fun to see the Mathis show and meet some of his friends there. I had danced with my date and his friend. Then I yelled down the table, "Look who just walked in!"

Johnny Mathis walked right by me, smiled, and said "Hello". I turned back to the group and said, "Wow! He can eat crackers in my bed any time." (That was also the title of a popular song at that time.) With that, my date announced that we were leaving, saying he thought he had gone out with a girl with class.

I said, "Good grief, can't you take a joke?" He couldn't and practically pushed me out the door. I was so upset because I was anxiously looking forward to the Johnny Mathis show, but didn't want to make a scene in front of his friends. When we got into his car, he drove like a madman, hitting some dips in the road so hard, my head hit the roof of his car and then hit the car seat so hard that my earring broke and caused my ear lobe to bleed.

The next day, one of his friends called to say that they had wished I could have stayed and they would have taken me home. But things happened so fast and they were all in shock over our quick departure from the club. They also warned me to be careful, because they had seen some strange behavior from him. They told me they had hired a black lady to clean their apartments and one of my "date's" socks turned up missing. This made him so angry that he walked up behind her, grabbed her arms, and kneed her in the buttocks. I knew I could never get serious with someone who showed such anger and disrespect for another human being.

In the 50's, when we gals had a date we would take what we called MAD MONEY and stick it in our bras; usually a five dollar bill. If we got mad at our dates, or if they drank too much, we could call a cab and go home. We carried a little money in our evening bags also, just in case someone snatched our bags while we were dancing, we could always take care of ourselves.

The next night I went dancing with someone who owned an exclusive dress shop. He had graciously walked me to the door, and left. One minute later, someone was banging loudly on the door. Then the glass in the door was knocked out. I hurriedly called the police. While I was talking to the policeman, my date from the previous night called me on the phone. The policeman told me to answer it.

He asked what I was doing and I told him that I was talking to the policeman because someone knocked the glass out of the front door.

He said, "Send him over here. I am the one who did it. And if I ever see you again, I'll kill you!"

I told the policeman what he had said, but told him that he was probably angry when he saw someone else take me home. And I told them that he was probably drunk, because his friends let him know they didn't appreciate the way he acted the night before at the Johnny Mathis show. The policeman told me he had a partner outside the door, and they were going by to let him know they didn't want to see him around my place any more. He said either a gun or car tool was used to knock out the window, so be careful.

A week later this guy called again to see if I wanted to marry him. Now, I had studied enough psychology in college to know there was something not normal about this guy.

I said, "No way!"

He had the audacity to ask, "Why not?"

I said, "Since you asked, I'll tell you! First, I could never marry anyone who is so jealous they don't trust me dancing with his best friend. Another thing, here in Texas, we speak to everyone. If you think that our next thought is to jump in bed, you have a crazy, twisted mind! I will never be so controlled; forget you ever asked me!" I hung up.

He called back to say," I will kill you if I ever see you again!"

I said, "Do you think you have a problem? Within the last five minutes, you have wanted to marry me and to kill me!" The policeman said if you ever threaten me, all I have to do is call and they will take care of you themselves. So I won't bother you, if you won't bother me!"

I pretty well agree with Will Rogers who said, "I never met a man I didn't like." (Unless, of course, he wanted to kill me!)

I heard later that he had married his college sweetheart. A few months later his friends called to see if I was safe, and Ann told them

I had gone to California. He had vomited and accused his wife of trying to poison him.

By the time I got back home, they had called back and said he had been found in New Orleans where he had locked himself in a hotel room for about 20 days. He had food sent to his room, but he didn't bother to shave or go out. Finally, the police had to put him in a straight jacket, because he started fighting them. My biggest regret was that I never did get to see Johnny Mathis sing those beautiful songs, all because my date acted like a junkyard dog!

Meanwhile, when DeVera was busy with business, he would send Ronnie Shipman to do an exhibition with me. Ronnie was a good dancer, good looking, and a great showman. One night, a booking agent came to our table and wanted to book us at the Coconut Grove in California. Ronnie got excited at the offer, and of course, I enjoyed going to California for the summers, so I thought it might be fun. (A booking agent had seen DeVera and me dance the year before, and offered us a job in New York. He couldn't go because of his business so I decided this might be a good opportunity to dance somewhere besides in Dallas).

Ronnie took off for California to find an apartment and get organized. Ann and I were to follow in a couple of weeks after school was out for the summer. Ann had a friend who had an apartment to rent to us, so we didn't have to spend time looking for one.

Next thing I knew, Ronnie called and said he was in San Diego, not Los Angeles. He had been in the military reserve, and as soon as he left town and didn't show up for a military reserve meeting, he was immediately assigned into active duty. He was in the Navy!

He wanted me to drive down there and meet him at the Arthur Murray Dance Studio, which I did. He hoped that we could work in a few exhibitions, and when they would see us dance together, the

Arthur Murray Studio would offer me a job to teach there. However, my friends were in Los Angeles, so I declined the offer and went back there to have fun for the summer.

When rock music became popular, the big band music temporarily became a thing of the past, along with ballroom dancing. The dance studios either closed or were barely hanging on to stay open. DeVera closed his studios and moved to another state. I heard that he went back to his roots, so his children would have the opportunity of knowing their grandparents.

I went to Arthur Murray's in Dallas to dance for a few months but the magic was not the same. One dancer wanted me to team up with him to dance on the famous ship, "Queen Mary". He had it planned that we would teach dancing during the daytime, and do exhibitions at night. The plans he made were too structured for my way of living—I didn't want to be confined on a ship. Instead, I planned a trip to Mexico. The teachers in the studio asked me to pick up some steps on the new dance craze, Cha-Cha-Cha, and bring it back to the studio. I wasn't there five minutes until I saw that it was simply the Mambo put to triple rhythm. The Cha-Cha-Cha was a fun dance that many were enjoying at the time. It was the last of the ballroom dances.

Soon I became disenchanted with teaching dances that were going out of style, so I said my goodbyes to my dancing friends. I felt that I had done enough dancing to get it out of my system, and I was finally ready for the next phase of my life.

I am pleased to see that the television show "Dancing with the Stars", has brought back popularity to the ballroom dancing. It was reported on television that the dance studios have had an increase of 30 percent in their business since the television ballroom dancing show began.

Ann Priest's life story moved and inspired me because of her daring and romantic triumphs over adversity. In times of adversity, she would always tell us to "rise above it". She was a complete pleasure in the way she looked and dressed. She was always dressed in beautiful, very expensive clothes, far beyond anything I had ever worn.

Ann was the most beautiful woman I had ever met and I was not surprised when she became a director of the John Robert Powers Modeling Schools in Dallas and Houston. Her laughter would light up a room. Anyone who heard her laugh would never forget it. She was perfect for running a modeling school as she derived so much pleasure in giving people a make-over. She was always dressing me up in her bracelets and earrings. I sometimes wore one of her fancy hats to church.

India Ann (Punkin) was equally as beautiful as Ann and looked exactly like her. Punkin and I wore the same dress size, so we often wore each other's clothes. As Punkin left for college one fall, she remarked that she felt she was leaving half her wardrobe in Dallas (meaning my clothes). But after a semester at Oklahoma University, she decided to come back to Dallas. She had been in a car wreck, and was thrown out of the car. Her face, arms, and legs were badly skinned up and she looked like a mess. She wanted to come home to her mommy. A group of football players came to see her during the OU football weekend in Dallas. I cooked a bunch of baby-back ribs and a friend, Mrs. Davis, made a big potato salad, and they all sat on the couch, chairs, and floor to eat. But she had already decided not to go back to Oklahoma.

Meanwhile, I found the ideal man for her. I taught physical education with Robbie Taylor. He was a good looking guy who had black curly hair. He was anxious to meet Punkin, but I made him wait until her face healed, because I had already told him that she was the prettiest girl in Dallas.

She had been a contestant once in the Miss Texas Beauty Pageant. I wanted everything to be perfect. When I got home in the afternoons, I'd tell her about his outstanding humor and good looks.

When the time was right, I cooked a big pot of my famous Chicken Cacciatori. Rob later told me that when he walked in and saw the candle light, heard the soft music, and smelled the chicken and rice dinner, he knew he'd "been had" right then and there. Of course, Ann and I had our dates there too, so we tried to make it light and fun.

The following Christmas, Rob and India Ann were married and have lived happily ever since. Punkin's dad bought them a new house, for a wedding gift. He lived in the bachelor quarters at the back of India Ann's house until his death a few years later.

Robbie was one of my favorite friends because he really knew how to have a good time. He was also full of jokes. I still remember one he told me that was so funny, I still laugh just thinking about it.

There were a couple of hookers who were comparing recent dates. One said, "I was with a little guy the other night named Shorty, and would you believe when he got undressed, I noticed he had SHORTY tattooed on his private area. I got so disgusted, I put my clothes on and went home!"

The other hooker said, "Honey, you left too soon. What it said was: SHORTY, FROM WAXAHACHIE, TEXAS."

Oh sure,–everyone should try it at least once!

Mother: "Whatever makes you happy."

Norene and Howard

Fun in the sun–boating at Nassau Bay–a new way of life

Howard with Jeanie (dog)

Norene with Poncho (dog)

Chapter 8

A Move to the Houston Area:

Making a Long Story Short

My friend, Ann Priest, was successful in directing the John Robert Powers Modeling School in Dallas. Now she had the opportunity to also direct the Houston Powers Modeling School. She wanted me to spend the summer with her in Houston. I would open the school in the mornings, answer the phone, and make appointments until she arrived.

Not only did Ann direct the modeling school, she also took a personal interest in the young girls who came in for the course. The school had many teachers, but it was just her way of making everyone feel special. It was also her nature to do and say things that would help each girl identify and accomplish her goals.

I would often listen to her talking to the girls. She would say things like: "There is so much more to gain from the course than just good grooming, applying make-up correctly, caring for your wardrobe, and learning to walk and sit gracefully." She stressed that a perfectly groomed woman is like a picture. Neglect of any one thing can ruin the picture.

From pages so yellow and faded, I'm having to use a magnifying glass to read, it will give you an idea of how she was, and how she tried so sincerely to help others.)

Personality Rules:

1. No matter how well you stack up on the good side of personality, do not be satisfied. The minute you stop growing you cease to be interesting.
2. Avoid inferiority complexes as well as superiority complexes, as both show too much thought of yourself.
3. If you think you have bad qualities, do not indulge in self pity. Do not try to copy another individual, but develop what you have to the best of your ability.

Charm is the power that you have over other people, and the ability to make them happy and at ease in your presence.

1. Give compliments sincerely.
2. Be understanding with others.
3. Don't pity, but respect their point of view.
4. Don't look down on anyone. Look up to everyone and tell them how wonderful they are.

5. Be tactful without hurting his/her feelings when correcting someone.
6. Be witty. Wit is a natural gift and everyone can be clever.

Conversation:

1. Be sure "comebacks" or jokes come with conversations. Tell only clean jokes. Don't make them too long or drawn out.
2. It's not what you say, but how you say it that is important.
3. Be mentally equipped by associating with quick thinkers.
4. Respect and look up to the other person. Forget about yourself, and be interested in the other person.
5. Be simple and truthful. Falsehood is complicated.
6. Be unselfish. Be silent when someone else has something to say.
7. Be dramatic and avoid monotony. Express emotion with your face. You can practically tell a story with your eyes.

Wow! You might say that anyone can read that out of a book. If you do, you have a good self-help book. But what I'm talking about is the true nature of Ann Priest. This is how she was all the time!

As I went through boxes of old pictures, trying to find one of Ann, I came across a poem which I had written about her.

Intellectual Annie

She's a proper Southern lady,
With a sophisticated air–
"We must do this, we must do that
Before someone will care."

With exceptional moral character
She set out to catch her prey–
But first, she must prepare herself
In a special kind of way.

She studied Cosmic forces–
The secret of its power,
Then a study in mental physics
To be used at the proper hour.

Through years of trial and error
She learned from God above;
Happiness lies, not in possession and power,
But in the gift and return of love.

So she set aside her other books;
Studies love with a philosophical view
Her eyes showing a new radiance and content;
She goes out to buy something new.

Spending hours getting primped and powdered;
Artistically adorned for the day;
One look at the man with encouraging smiles,
She knows she has caught her prey.

While absorbed in many entanglements of love;
Studies men with a psychological approach
In the thrills of love and happiness
Finds Biology has helped her the most!

One day, after I had opened the Power's School in Houston, a good looking guy walked in and was asking for some models to be used for the upcoming Houston Boat Show. We had coffee and talked until Ann arrived. I found out that he sold yachts and cruisers near the Space Center (between Houston and Galveston). His name was Howard Laravea. We dated that summer, and before I went back to Dallas to teach that fall, he asked me to marry him.

Of course, Ann wanted me to move to the Houston area, so we could be together more often. She told me, "Everyone should try marriage at least once!"

She had tried it four times, and had told me it was just a matter of exchanging one set of problems for another. Myrtice was taking a "wait and see" attitude. She had consoled me through two broken engagements while I lived in Dallas. On each occasion we had gone out and spent a lot of money buying dresses and accessories before I changed my mind.

She sent me a cartoon out of a magazine where the sales lady was saying to the girl who was looking at a wedding dress, "My advice is to snap it up now while its on sale, and then look for a husband."

I sent a cartoon back to Myrtice that had a gal sitting at a bar, and saying, "When I get ready to get married, I'll just look them over and say, " eeny, meeny, miney, MONEY!"

Howard came to Dallas a couple of times, to try to convince me to get married. My motto was, "NEVER GIVE UP ANYTHING YOU HAVE, UNLESS YOU CAN EXCHANGE IT FOR SOMETHING BETTER. I loved my job teaching in Dallas, but decided that perhaps having a job and a husband would be even better. As soon as I was hired in the Clear Creek Independent Schools, I started making plans for the big move.

Curtis and Myrtice's wedding gift to us was to host the wedding. We got married in their church in Arlington on December 22, 1962. People thought I would have a problem settling down to one person, but I didn't. Marriage was a serious step for me.

However, it turned out in our three and a half years of marriage, that Howard was born to be a playboy, He always had to stop and drink beer with his buddies before he came home. One night, I cooked his favorite dish, meat loaf.

He said, "Here I am eating meat loaf, and the dog is down there eating a t-bone steak."

I said, "That's your meal from last night when you were probably too drunk to find your way home."

He knocked my chair over with me still sitting in it. My doctor put me on tranquilizers and told me that staying married was ruining my health. My body chemistry changed, and I almost died in the hospital due to a kidney infection. I realized my back was giving me some problems, but I concluded that it was because of some tumbling I had done with my gym class. When I started having chills, I stopped by the doctor's office on the way home, and he said I had a 104-degree temperature, and to go straight to the hospital.

Ann came down from Houston, and by the time she got there, my temperature had gone to 106 degrees. I kept passing out, and when I would wake up, I'd ask for another blanket, even though I already had thirteen blankets on me. The doctor told me later that I almost died.

One night, I found Howard spending the night on a boat with a married lady. I called her the next day and told her I needed to talk with her. I told her that I might be getting a divorce, and that if she would tell me everything, I would not involve her. She had a husband and a couple of small children.

She told me even more than I expected. She had convinced her husband that she was drinking and playing cards with her girl friends. So they restricted her from driving and had her spend the night. Consequently, her husband was also being told a bunch of lies.

I thought I was about to have a nervous breakdown, so I called my priest for consultation. Can you imagine asking my Episcopal priest to meet me at the church during a snow storm? He must have thought I was nuts. He told me that I didn't have any kind of good marriage and to get out! Having given up my job in Dallas to move down there, I didn't want to give up on what should have been beautiful. Since I didn't file for divorce right away, I could have waited until the snow melted to call my priest!

I called the priest again and asked if he would come to our apartment and talk with Howard. When he arrived, Howard locked himself in the bathroom, so there was no communication. The priest left, never to return!

Howard, with all his charm, said he would do better, so I let him stay. Consequently, I told him that I could not, and would not continue to live his life style. I never knew when, or if he would come home. After three years, I filed for divorce. He asked if I would marry him again, and I said that enough is enough. We could be friends, but no more dating. I "sure-as-hell" wouldn't consider marrying him again.

Howard later married a girl who resembled me. One day he called to tell me that his sister had died, so I went to the funeral home. As luck would have it, we drove up at the same time. He opened the door for his new wife and for me. As we walked in, the wife of the funeral director said, "Well, I know you've got to be Howard's wife's sister!"

I said, "Guess again, how about ex-wife?"

She said, "Oh dear, me and my big mouth!"

I was rather amused to look at her and see my "look-alike". I wanted to ask, "What were you thinking?"

Several years later, after I had moved back to North Texas, Jeannie called to tell me that he had died of a heart attack. At the time he was again divorced and had been making plans to marry still another lady. He was charming and good looking, but what bothered me about him was that he would lie when the truth would sound better. He tried to withdraw my life savings from my Credit Union account. He sold my car on which I had made every payment, and did many other underhanded things that he should have known could not be forever hidden.

He withdrew money from the bank account quicker that I could put it in. He did not tell me about the withdrawals so I couldn't keep the books accurately. I was so disgusted I didn't want to carry his name, so I returned to my maiden name. I was from a family with unquestionable integrity.

I will never understand why people choose to lie. Even what some people call a little white lie is not acceptable to my past training. A lie is a lie, no matter what color or size you give it.

Once I have heard someone lie, I start doubting anything that person may say. I recognize the fact that unless someone is under oath, they are under no obligation to tell the truth. They can politely say something like, "I really don't like to discuss my personal business with anyone, so maybe we could discuss you instead."

I really don't feel obligated to tell anything or everything to anybody. If someone gets angry, so be it. It's better than losing your integrity by not being honest.

In the old days, there was a saying that a person was as good as his word. Instead of contracts, many deals were made over a handshake and a cup of coffee. In our household, if we told someone we would do something, I'll guaranDAMNtee you, that we were compelled to keep our word. It wouldn't have been acceptable to change our mind. You are either honest or a liar. Enough said! For the most part I like everyone, but there are a few that I would not want to do business with—much less marry!

While I was still married, I went boating with Howard. He told me he needed to take a few prospects out for a boat ride and asked if I would come along. I remember this lovely young couple who were attending college in Austin. They didn't socialize much with others on the boat, but seemed to enjoy being with each other. He seemed very attracted to his wife, and playfully pulled her down on his knee and kissed her a couple of times.

I thought to myself how nice it must be to get all that attention. I do remember his complaining a couple of times about having a splitting headache. A couple of days later, Howard told me to turn on the television. This guy had killed his wife and mother and then climbed to the dome of a building at Texas University, and started shooting at people. He shot forty-three people. Fifteen died, including his wife and mother, before he was killed by the police. His name was Charles Whitman. I wondered what in the world would get a person that screwed up. An autopsy showed that he had a brain tumor.

I always try to make the best of a situation, so after the divorce, I got back in circulation. There was a saying, "Do you dare to be different?" I not only dared, it was my nature to be different. Once I told my principal about some of the good times I had experienced in Mexico because of the Latin dancing. The gigolos wanted to dance with me.

My principal and his wife (the Puckett's) had been dance instructors after the war, so we had a lot of common interests. His best friend,

Johnny Ghirardi, was also a good dancer. We went dancing almost every weekend in the Houston area. During the Christmas holidays, we all drove to Mexico and had the time of our lives!

When I lived across the street from the Houston Space Center, Jean Williams was my best friend. She was a gourmet cook, and often invited me to eat with her. When she would have to be away, I would keep her little white poodle, Pancho. Once when she went to Europe, I had become so attached to her poodle, that I cried when she came to pick him up. She was such a sweet friend and gave me a little black poodle. I had never received such a wonderful gift from a friend, and I was speechless! I named her Jeanie, after my friend, Jeanie.

I entered Jeanie (the dog) in a dog contest. We were to dress our animal in a costume. I made a two-piece bikini of red silk, covered with red net and tiny blue, yellow, and white flowers. She also wore a red hat with tiny flowers. Jeanie won the trophy that eventful day! What was so cute, was that she turned to the runner-up and they touched noses, like they were kissing! Everyone laughed! It was like "Miss America", dog style!

A funny thing happened one day in gym class. I had the second grade girls on the exercise mats and was demonstrating and explaining how to do a head stand without using the wall.

I said "squat down and put your knees on the outside of your elbows. Then lower your head so that it will be about a foot above the hands, making an imaginary triangle. Slowly, raise the feet until they are straight up in the air. Then slowly bend the knees and come back down."

As I stood up, the children went into laughing hysterics. There was my wig still on the mat!

One of the little girls said, "For a split second, Miss Nygaard, I thought you'd lost your head!"

Living at the Space Center was quite an experience. I enjoyed knowing the astronauts and teaching their children. Many had boats, and we would cruise right up to their houses and visit from the water's edge. Red Adair and his wife were acquaintances who also had a yacht. (He was the world-known firefighter. Even his boat had a lot of red on it.) We often went by boat to eat at some very interesting places on the water's edge.

I took a course on boating while I lived there and made a perfect score on my test. Sometimes I would handle the boat, but I never did buy one. I knew that my relaxed days of boating were coming to an end, as my thoughts started turning to my friends and family who lived in the North Texas area. It was just a matter of time before I applied for a job, and make arrangements for another move.

Norene-a time to retire-1984

Myrtice retired, 1981

A hobby & business—arranging silk flowers

Do blonds really have more fun?
No, but it sure helps to cover the
gray–around 50 and after.

Custom Designed Silk Flower
Arrangements For Less

Norene's Floral

144

Myrtice & Norene–celebrating in Hong Kong

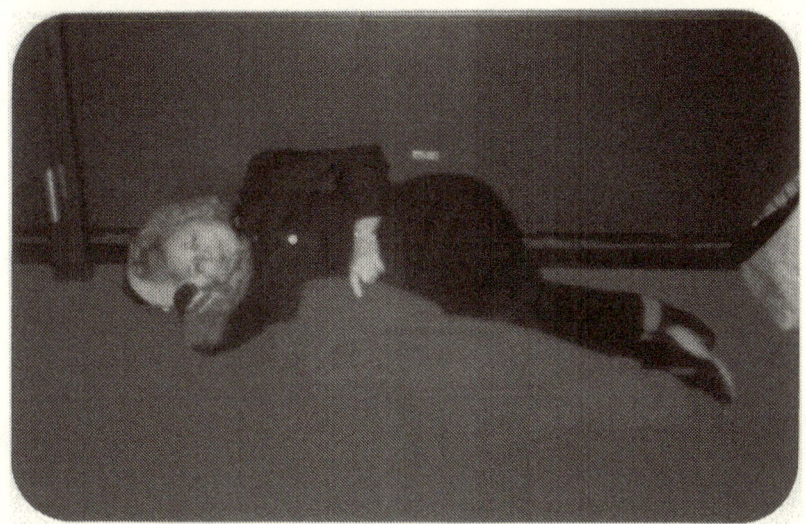

Missed another plane–slept on the floor
at the Los Angeles Airport.

Chapter 9

Back to North Texas - My Roots

I moved back to the North Texas area between Dallas and Fort Worth, in the summer of 1971, and started teaching for the Hurst-Euless-Bedford Independent School District. I remember the first day I drove up to the Midway Park Elementary School and saw some black children playing on the playground. It was the first time in my 25 years of teaching that I had ever taught African-American children. I was absolutely intrigued by them. I even liked the relaxed way they walked.

Then one rainy day when we couldn't go outside, I turned on some music and you should have seen them dance! My first thought was, "There's my next PTA Program." What natural rhythm they had! If I had not already had a day job, I would probably have been preparing them for the Apollo Theater!

They liked me, too. There was a Tom Thumb grocery store between where they lived in Mosier Valley and where I lived in the Sotogrande Apartments. I would often see some of the children there on weekends. When one of them would see me, he would yell out, "Hey, everybody, Miss Nygaard is here!" The children would come running.

Shoppers in the store would say, "I'll bet you are a school teacher".

One weekend, they had an all-day festival at their church, and they begged me to come to their church that Sunday. I did, and as I walked in, the minister welcomed me, and the congregation clapped with joy. We had a big lunch and had home made ice cream for dessert. I will always cherish that special Sunday we spent together. I like the way black folks get excited in church. They clap, they shout, they dance! How wonderful it must be to be able to express yourself so freely!

One day, one of the little black boys came up to my desk and said, "Miss Nygaard, I have a really big request to make."

I said, "What can I do for you?"

He said, "I just love your beautiful blond hair, and I was wondering if you would let me touch it, as I have never touched blond hair before!"

I said, "I'll make a deal with you. I will let you touch my hair if you will let me touch your hair, because you see, I have never touched black, curly hair".

He said, "Deal!" I let him go first. He seemed to have so much fun running his fingers through my hair, telling me how nice and soft it was. Then it was my turn. He kneeled in front of me so I could reach the top of his head.

I said, "I like the way your hair feels, too! It's so nice and soft and cushioned. Somehow, I expected it to feel more like a Brillo Pad!"

He got so tickled, he fell over backwards, and rolled on the floor laughing.

Another day, one of the little black girls came to school with a new hair-do.

I said, "Someone has sure done a pretty job on your hair. It has little braids and colorful balls on the end of each one. Wow! You look beautiful!"

She said, "My grandma said I look just like a little black Christmas tree!"

The children would go to church on Wednesday nights, and the next day they would tell me all about the service. The children were always so excited when they would tell me anything, and I hope that feeling of joy has stayed with them through the years. I sometimes wondered if kids were there to teach me or to learn from me. It's no wonder God loves the little children.

During the 70's there was a television show called "Roots" which showed all about the beginning of slavery. I encouraged the class to watch the program so we could discuss it the following day. The program was on twice a week for two weeks. It showed how terrible the black people had been treated. They were chained and brought to the United States from Africa. One of the little girls had just told me that someone had made fun of her because she was black.

At the time, I was in the middle of a class instruction, and was so busy with a lesson that I just said something like, "Just rise above it, and don't let it bother you." The truth was, I didn't quite know how to approach the problem. This movie gave me the opportunity to get word to the class on how they should treat everyone. I got them in our reading circle and made sure I was sitting by this little black girl who had been rejected by her classmates.

I explained how mean some of the white people had been. We can right a wrong by loving all our classmates and respecting everyone we meet, no matter what color they are.

I said, "Always remember, that one person is no better than another one, so if you see someone picking on someone of another color, let them know that their behavior is not acceptable. Then go up and hug the person who's heart is breaking, and be their best friend, so they won't continue to hurt." With that, I hugged the little black girl next to me. After a few talks like that, I noticed the other kids were playing with her on the playground, and she actually became a leader before the end of the year. We must never underestimate the power of our actions. With a small gesture, you can change a person's life -- for better or for worse.

Of course , you don't have to be so dead serious every time a child gets in an argument with another child. When I was a Physical Education teacher, often, there were fights on the playground. Sometimes, I could turn it around by saying something like, "Seems to me that both of you owe each other an apology." And if they stood there like they were not about to be the first to apologize, I'd say something like, "If you don't apologize and shake hands, I might make you hug each other!" By then, we were all laughing. Then I would add, "You'd better hurry, or I might make you kiss each other!" By then, even they were laughing, and shaking hands–and they were ready to go back into the game. To me, this seemed like a better way to settle differences, rather than the traditional way of piling anger on top of anger.

We get so busy adding up our problems that we forget to count our blessings. God put us in each others lives to hopefully impact one another in a positive way. Now, years later, when I see them at McDonalds or at a grocery store, they still run up and hug me like they did when they were second graders. After many years, I met the girl that I hugged in the reading circle. We were at a favorite steak house, and she came to my table and told me that I had no idea of the impact that I had made on her life, and we hugged and cried together. When a teacher knows she spent her life doing a job that paid almost nothing, these are the moments that makes it all worthwhile.

My best friend in this area was Victoria (Vickie) Copeland. We lived in the same apartment complex, and were both second grade teachers in the same school, in the same room! We could look across the room at each other and know what the other one was thinking. She had a free spirit—like me! She had a boy friend who said to her, "All you think about is FUN, FUN, FUN!" We had many laughs over his remarks. She was good at planning parties for the residents of the apartment complex where she had moved. Our pupils told us that they had never had teachers like us in their entire lifetime–and they were second graders!

Once we went to Ringling Brothers, Barnum and Bailey Circus in Fort Worth. We jotted down ideas for a PTA program. A month or two later, we had a boy stand before the audience and announce, "Welcome to the Greatest Show on Earth!" I remember making about 20 clown costumes after school for students whose mother didn't sew. As the crowd came into the auditorium, my dad was at the entrance playing the accordion. He had on a clown hat and a little boy did a jig to his music. We had clowns going up and down the aisles selling peanuts and popcorn to help defray the expenses of the costumes and other props.

Dad moved to the front of the stage and I did a jig. Then Vickie led the group into the auditorium to the music of the Trinity High School Band playing, "The Circus Parade March". The children marched in and took a seat on the floor at the front of the stage. All the second grade sang, "Goodbye, Mommy, Goodbye Daddy". The class also sang "I want to be a Lion Tamer", as the lion tamer popped his whip for the lions to do their tricks.

While the band played, "That's Entertainment", a tight rope walker and acrobatic clowns came onto the stage. Miss Copeland's dog, Tosha, danced out on the stage on her hind legs and jumped through the hula hoop. We also had hobo's singing, "Side By Side", a girl doing a tap dance, tricycle clowns, jugglers, the Charleston "Flapper Tappers", and playful clowns doing tumbling tricks on the gym mats.

I'd venture to say it was probably the best PTA program those parents had ever seen, as well as the best performance of the children. The music teacher, Molly Tuley, taught the songs. Our art teacher, Vercile Jordan, had taught the children water-color painting for the covers of the printed programs which were handed out at the door. Children always remember the PTA programs they were in, and talk about them for years.

One thing I liked about planning programs for children, was how it brought out their personalities. One little Mexican girl, who had been very shy around her classmates, did a Mexican dance in her beautiful costume.

All the children suddenly started paying attention to her, and she was no longer a shy little wall flower! When I taught some Mexican dances, I made her my assistant, which gave her even more confidence. I remember one PTA program in which a little crippled boy sang and played his guitar to the "Gamblers Song". He brought the house down. All the programs we did scored a few points with the parents, too.

Children never, ever, forget the singing and dancing they did while they were in elementary school. I always found that when we could make school fun and interesting for the children, it would reflect favorably on their grades. I loved how much the children had grown academically, from the time they came to me at the beginning of the school year, and how much they had accomplished by the end of the year. I was always so proud of them. They were like different children, and the test grades showed it.

One year, I had a very smart class and because of the extremely high grades, the principal decided to have half of them skip a grade. By encouraging children, it is amazing how smart they can become. When they see the confidence you have in them, you can almost see their growth and development from one day to the next. Children want to please their teachers, they want to learn, and they love praise just like everyone else. So dish it out teachers (and parents), and believe me, they will deliver and make you proud.

I always got so deeply involved in the books I read to the children. I lived the story so completely that when I was reading a chapter a day of "Charlotte's Web" to the second grade class, I found it interesting that Charlotte, a spider, had such good friends like the pig and other farm animals. At lunch time, one of the second grade teachers would be in charge of the lunch room while another one would read to the children. It was my week to read. I told the teachers that Charlotte was going to die the next day and that I needed to swap duties, because I knew when Charlotte dies, that I will start crying–then the class would do likewise. One of the teachers took my spot for the day. She said they got teary-eyed and one of them said, "We'd better not tell Miss Nygaard that Charlotte died, because she loved her so much–and she will cry! I just know she will!"

I joined a health club when I moved to the North Texas area, and eventually joined the Hurst Recreational Club, where they offered many classes. First, I took a tap dancing class. Later, I signed up for a harem (belly dancing) class. When the first and second grade teachers had the weekly team meeting, I talked some of them into joining the class with me. We had to give our phone numbers at work, never expecting them to be used. One day, it started snowing and sleeting as school was about to be dismissed for the day.

The principal announced on the speaker, "The teachers who are involved in a 'certain class' at the Hurst Recreation Club will not go tonight, as all classes have been canceled."

The teachers stuck their heads into my room and each with a big smile on her face said, "I don't believe I want to go to the office to check out today!"

I said, "Just don't swivel your hips too much and maybe Mr. May won't know you are one of the dancers."

At the end of every year, the teachers would go to Fort Worth for an evening of fun at Joe-T. Garcia's Mexican Restaurant. They always expected me to entertain them with a few Mexican dances. There was a guitar player there, Juan Hernandez, who was a good showman and knew how to flirt with his eyes and smile. After a margarita or two, it proved to be fun for all of us.

As I danced, I clicked the castanets. Others brought their noise-making instruments from home, and got in the act, too! I knew we were having a good time when I saw my team leader with straws sticking out of her nostrils!

I always thought it was a little fun to slightly shock friends. The teachers were in a faculty meeting for the purpose of changing our school health insurance plan. We were filling out the application forms and were to check, (a) single (b) married(c) divorced (d) widowed. I said, "I wonder if I have time to run out and get married, so I can check ALL OF THE ABOVE."

Mr. May said, "Norene, we are wondering why you aren't married. Is there something you have against men or marriage?"

I said, "Frankly, I can't think of anything more boring than to wake up with the same man in bed with me for the next 50 years!" The faculty laughed, so I added, "That didn't come out quite like I intended. Right now, when I wake up each morning, there's a big black, long-legged poodle in my bed. And for 14 years before this dog, I had a little short-legged black poodle in my bed. So let's put it this way, I have never been bored with a dog! And surprising as this may sound, they think I'm perfect! Now, if any of you sleep with someone who is always happy with you, no matter what you say or do, stand up and take a bow. (Everyone laughed, but no one stood up.) I do believe I rest my case!"

The car accident and the boat accident had left my back structurally damaged. Recurring pain was now causing health problems in the form of arthritis. Being unable to exercise as I had been accustomed to was also causing a weight problem. Finally in 1983, I had a back operation, which seemed to result in more pain than comfort.

I decided to retire in 1984, after 38 years of teaching school. There were six parties given in my honor. Even my principal, Mr. May, gave me a party at my favorite steak house, and paid for all the teachers dinners.

The teachers told me that at the last PTA meeting, I would be presented with a plaque in honor of my 38 years of teaching, and another one for the 13 years with the HEB schools. I always liked to joke around a little, so I told the teachers, that when I would go forward to receive my gift, I was going to stand there and sing, "You Can Take This Job and Shove It".

I think about half of the teachers were really worried that I might burst into song!

I had planned to recite this poem at the last PTA meeting, but I was already on the verge of tears, so I accepted the plaques that were presented to me and sat down.

A Teacher Prays

There goes my last wee problem out the door;
The room is strangely silent now at four.
I need no resting place to kneel and pray;
The Master Teacher can't be far away.

Dear Jesus, keep my little ones from harm
Until a Mother's tender, loving arm,
Encircles each small wonder with joy
And closely hugs a rumpled girl or boy.

And now, dear Lord, forgiveness I implore
For harsh and bitter words I spoke
Before I knew how soon blue eyes can fill with tears,
And rosy little cheeks can pale with fears.

Through years of service, 'till life's clock strikes four
And homeward bound, the teacher shuts the door
And hurries gladly toward her joys to be
Led by a little child, at last to Thee.

The teachers recommended my name to be put in the "Notable Women of Texas 1984-85 Edition". I happened to call it "Notorious Women of Texas", and my sister said, "Yeah, that's more like it!" I felt especially honored over this recognition, and pleased to find that I was in the same edition as our past woman governor, the late Ann Richards.

During the last few years of my teaching career, I became interested in making silk flower arrangements for home decorating, as they had become very popular at the time. At first, I made many of the flowers, but because of my limited time, I decided to buy ready-made flowers for my arrangements. I signed up with the State of Texas as a small business entrepreneur, so I could buy the flowers wholesale. Every weekend, I would go to Fort Worth Floral or to San Lorenzo's in Dallas to the wholesale houses, and get a week's supply of silk flowers.

I would work on the arrangements at night and put them in the teachers lounge. They would all be sold by the end of the day. An antique shop owner where I bought many vases, wanted me to put some of the arrangements in their shop to make their place pretty and colorful. I also put some in an exclusive dress shop. I had many beautiful arrangements, and again, I knew this was a gift from God. It all came together so easily for me, and people would tell me mine were the prettiest arrangements they had ever seen.

Certain things can have a big effect on people and they not even realize it. When I taught school in Dallas, I worked in the physical education department. The teachers loved for me to do their PTA programs each month because I could teach singing and dancing to the students. Several years later when the kids had a day off between semesters, they would come to the school where I had taught fourth through eighth grades. They said they still talk about all the programs in which I had them to perform. They vowed always to remember it. They told me I was so different from any other teacher they had ever known.

Twenty years after I had left Dallas to spend seven years at the Space Center and thirteen years teaching for the Hurst-Euless-Bebford Schools district, I received a letter from a former pupil. I was informed that the old James Bowie School in Dallas was going to be demolished and replaced with a new building. A reunion was being planned and I was invited.

My first thought was that no one would remember me, but since they wanted everyone who had been connected with that school to be there, I decided to go. There was a program planned, followed by lunch in the lunchroom. They had the teachers stand as they called our names.

The speaker said, "And the next teacher was every boy's first love. We all lined up to kiss her goodbye from the time we were in the fourth grade, and we were still doing it in the eight grade - Miss Nygaard!"

Everyone screamed and clapped! I stood up, waved, then threw a big kiss to the crowd. What a wonderful feeling. I was sitting next to Dr. Walker, and he reached over and patted me on the hand. He had been a principal in that school, before he became the Assistant Superintendent of the Dallas Schools. I was so glad I had gone to Dallas that day.

Myrtice, who had retired two years prior to my retirement, was doing extensive traveling all over the world. She suggested I go with her and her traveling group to Hong Kong for a couple of weeks to celebrate being retired. We had a good time, but on the way home there was a fire in the electrical system of the plane and we had to land in Japan and wait for another plane.

By the time we arrived in California, we had missed the flight schedule, so we had to wait until morning to leave to come home. We were offered a room at a hotel, but I suggested we stay there so we wouldn't miss another plane. I put my sweater under my head and slept on the floor. Myrtice can sleep on a plane, even when it is on fire, but not me!

Later, a friend, Ann Stary, invited us to California to visit with her for a couple of weeks. She took us to some wonderful places. We saw the Crystal Cathedral one day. She also took us to the stage show, "Best Little Whore House in Texas". We went to Las Vegas on our way home. What happens in Vegas, stays in Vegas—especially my money!

Daddy's health began to deteriorate after breaking his hip in a fall while he was mowing his yard. He later had heart trouble which added to his problems, so Myrtice and I spent many hours with him. He lived in Grand Prairie, which is between Hurst and Dallas, so I was thankful that we could all be together often. During the next two years, we had many good times together.

Eventually, he had to go to a nursing home. However, we would continue our daily trips to visit him. Then we got involved by helping other patients during their meal times. Myrtice and I would assist the patients by getting them more water or coffee and Noran often helped by pushing them back to their rooms. At Christmas time, Myrtice fixed a sack of cookies and candy for each of the patients at the nursing home. I made a small silk flower arrangement that was pinned to their pillow. They appreciate everything: a handshake, a smile, a little gift. Little children from a nearby school came by to sing Christmas carols, and asked the patients to sing along with them.

Myrtice hosted several birthday parties for Dad at her home. His nieces and nephews brought him treats and gifts. It was easy to see that little things meant a lot to him. At his last party, I asked him if he was worn out by the end of the day.

He said, "Why no—I've had the time of my life!"

He was almost 93 at the time of his death, and was so ready to be with the Lord. He died at Christmas time, and since he loved singing Christmas carols, we sang carols at his funeral. Our cousin, Kenneth Surley and his wife, Pat, also sang a beautiful hymn.

My cousin and her husband, Martha and Fred Schuster, invited us to their home on Christmas Day. That became an annual tradition. We enjoyed being with our paternal relatives at Christmas time. We meet with our maternal relatives on Thanksgiving Day, at our cousin's home, Jennie Mae Jenson, in Waco. We also have a family reunion with them during the summertime.

Since I retired, Myrtice and Noran have taken me to Mexico three times, but not to dance. We have gone to a medical clinic there for me to get some shots, therapy, and pills for arthritis. Now, I play on Dad's accordion the song, "The Old Gray Mare, She Ain't What She Used to Be" (many long years ago).

Myrtice and Curtis Larson Elementary School
Arllington, Texas

Daddy

Aunt Minnie

Noran

Mother

Me, Dad, & King Olav V
of Norway

Chapter 10

Unforgettable Characters in my Life

Aunt Minnie

You may have noticed by now that this book isn't just about ME, ME, ME. I am who I am because of the impact others have made upon my life. One of the most outstanding people I have ever known was my Aunt Minnie Bertelson. She was my sponsor (godmother) when I was baptized. She assisted the doctor when he came to our farm at midnight to help Mother give birth to my twin brother and me.

I always thought I should write about her for the Readers Digest when they published the article, "The Most Unforgettable Character I Ever Met". What made her so outstanding was the charity and love she gave to so many people. She helped the doctor give birth to about half of the young people in her town, even though she was not a registered nurse. She taught school to the other half of the people because she was a certified teacher.

Most everyone called her "Aunt Minnie" or "Miss Minnie" because of the impact she had on their lives. She taught Sunday School, and also found time to take people who were sick to Clifton, because there was no longer a doctor in Cranfills Gap. Those who needed to go to the grocery store, and couldn't because they were either sick or without a car, knew they could count on her to look after their needs.

When we were little children, she would call Mother on the phone and say she was coming to see us. We were so happy, and would sing the old song, "She'll Be Coming Around the Mountain When She Comes". She would bring something special like a big piece of roast, a pie, or a cake. She was a good cook, and also enjoyed company.

When we had late ball games at school, some of our friends would join us and spend the night with her. The boys would sleep upstairs, and the girls would sleep downstairs. I recall the delicious smell of the bacon frying as we got up the next morning.

Later in life, when my mother was alone, and not in good health, Aunt Minnie insisted Mom move in with her and Uncle Bernt. From then on, we always knew we had a place to call home. She lived in a big two story house, and if we didn't go home often, Aunt Minnie would call us and say, "I'm cooking a bunch of things today, and it sure would be fun if we had someone with whom to share all this food for the weekend." Her heart was big, and her house was always open to everyone.

We went to town one day to put gas in the car, and a couple drove up. They asked Aunt Minnie if she knew of a place to eat.

She replied, "I sure do—follow me".

She already had lunch ready, so she fed them. Now, how often do you see that kind of hospitality given to strangers?

Once, when I was in Dallas, she called me when school was out, and suggested I bring enough clothes to stay for a couple of weeks. She said she would have a surprise for me when I would get there. She had told the minister that she thought I would teach the beginning Confirmation Class in Vacation Bible School that summer. How could I say "No" to someone like her. Classes were only until noon, so we could go shopping in Meridian or Hamilton in the afternoon. Some days we would just stay at home and rest. Of course, she knew she was making my mother very happy also by having me come to her house for a couple of weeks.

When I had problems, I always knew I could go to my "godmother", Aunt Minnie, for advice and comfort. It always bothered me when I'd make such a "mell of a hess" out of my life. It took a couple of years of having a near nervous breakdown before I told my family about my marriage difficulties, because I kept thinking we could work things out. Only my priest, my doctor, and friend, Jeanie, knew what I was going through. I finally wrote Aunt Minnie a letter to let her know what a mess I'd made of my life.

I still have the short note that she wrote in response. "We look not back, God knows the fruitless efforts, the wasted hours, the sinning, the regrets.

We leave them all with Him who blots out the record, and graciously forgives, and then forgets."   Aunt Minnie

"How is the new car? When are you coming?"

It was as though she described what God would have done; forgive and forget. Then she would go on to something completely new, never to question me or bring up the subject again. Like God, she accepted my faults and went on enjoying our time together.

Aunt Minnie was married to Bernt Bertelson, who owned the barber shop in Cranfills Gap. During the Christmas holidays, he set up a table in the front window of the barber shop, and sold fire crackers, sparklers, and Roman candles. As children, we enjoyed all the noise and beauty of it all.

He often entertained us by playing his violin. He was from a musical family. His brothers played the guitar and his sister played the piano and organ at our church. He also played the saxophone with us in the Cranfills Gap High School band. I always sat next to him as I also played a saxophone.

My dad–Otto Nygaard

Besides being a farmer and a rancher, Dad also was interested in big machinery, such as was used in road building. To make extra money, he drove the big combines in the West Texas wheat fields. During World War II, he worked at North American Aircraft in Grand Prairie, Texas, building fighter airplanes. During the summertime, while still on the farm, he worked with the steam engine and separator during the threshing season.

Unbeknownst to him, many years later, this word got to Iowa and he was invited to a State Fair and Thresher Reunion. Myrtice flew with him as he had never been on a plane. At the airport he excused himself to go to the rest-room. As he returned, Myrtice said he was laughing hysterically. She asked him what was so funny and he replied, "Here I am, an 80 year old man, and this is the first time I've ever had to pay to pee."

As they landed in Iowa he wanted to go shopping to buy an engineer's cap. The next day he captivated an audience by telling them of his work experiences. Myrtice said he delivered a message of greeting as if he were an ambassador of the Dallas/Ft. Worth metroplex, inviting them to come see the Dallas Cowboys, Texas Rangers, and the Six Flags of Texas. He was also excited by all the attention he received when he drove the steam engine in the official parade.

My dad used to joke that he was blind in one eye, and couldn't see out of the other. He had, in fact, gone blind in his left eye, and as a result of impaired vision was hit by an oncoming car at a stop sign. He didn't like to skip Sunday School and church services, so I offered to take him while his car was being repaired. I found out that he had really studied his lesson.

The minister was the teacher of the adult class. Daddy answered the first three questions. When the minister asked the next one, Daddy remained quiet, as did the entire class. The teacher said, "Otto, don't you know the answer?"

He replied, "Sure, I just thought I should give someone else a chance to answer".

The teacher said, "Otto, I do believe you are the only one in my congregation who studied the lesson, so I will leave it for you to answer."

Dad said, "Well, then let me turn around a little so I can explain it to them". Everyone laughed.

It reminded me of the breakfast I had with him that morning. By the time he had read a passage from the Bible and said a prayer, the bacon and eggs were getting cold, but I knew better than to suggest we hurry to eat while it was hot.

I started asking him to pray for me about certain matters that needed God's attention. He always said "okay", until finally one day he said, "I will be glad to, but don't forget that God will hear your prayers just as quickly as he will hear mine".

I said, "Every time I come over here, you are reading the Bible, so I've decided you must have a straight line".

He laughed and told me that if I didn't have a straight line, I'd better invest a little more time to get one.

We had lots of laughs and good times in his last days. One day, he was trying to tell me something, and couldn't remember the word he wanted to use. He hit the table with his fist and said, "It makes me so mad when I can't remember a simple word, like people's names."

I said, "Maybe that's God's way of saying we don't have to be burdened with remembering every little thing anymore."

A big smile came across his face, and he said, "Well, I hadn't thought of it that way, (and looking up, said) thank you, God."

By now, he was in a wheel chair, and I asked him one day what was on his mind as I pushed him. He said, "It's like I am floating across the room."

I said, "Look at it this way, you spent your entire life working hard. Now, thank God, you don't have to work any more. From now on, it's a free ride!" He laughed as I pushed him to the "mess hall" for lunch.

My mother–Hannah Nygaard

I have already written so much about my mother in a previous chapter, so at this time, I will let everyone know the humorous side of her. My mother had a sense of humor that few knew about. Everyone thought of her as a very quiet lady. But I could name anyone (man or woman) and she could impersonate them exactly as they talked.

We knew one lady who acted a little "uppity", like she was above everyone else. Mother had complete control of the English language, but when she "mocked" this lady, she spoke using one grammatical error after another. She raised her eyebrows and pranced around like she was Mrs. Important. She spoke with a Norwegian brogue, but it sounded like she just got off the ship. The English was really chopped up, using "is" for "are", etc. It would crack me up! But I would tell her not to let them know she can mimic them, because they might think she is making fun of them. Little did I know that people who are this talented would be making millions these days for the like of her talent!

Mother was so skinny (she weighed less than 100 pounds), so I bought and persuaded her to wear a padded bra. I gave her a permanent and a new dress, and we went to church the next day. This little Norwegian lady came up to her as we were leaving church and said, "Hannah, you are looking so good. You know, you used to be so tin (thin)." As she spoke, she pounded her hands on her chest. When we got home, she told Aunt Minnie what the lady said, and using her Norwegian brogue, sounded just like the lady. We laughed until tears streamed down our cheeks.

One of mother's neighbors asked her if the farm was for sale. She jokingly said, "Yes, if I can keep the mineral rights."

"What did he say?" I asked.

She imitated him exactly by saying,

"Oh sh-- no! Oh sh-- no!"

I laughed so hard as it was the only time I ever heard her say a dirty word. The thought of anyone saying that to my mother made it even funnier because by nature, she was so quiet and reserved.

Mother was of Norwegian descent, as were most people in this small town. But with her schooling and years of teaching, she overcame talking with an accent, if she ever had it. I was there one weekend when a neighbor came to the door to tell them about a lady who had died.

I told mother that I didn't hear everything she said, so would she repeat it for me. So she said (with the Norwegian brogue) "Oh, my, have you heard that Olga died last night? Poor thing, she always complained, so it's good that she died. Oh my, she was hurting so bad, poor thing. It's good that she finally died!"

By the time Mother got through with her Norwegian way of telling it, we were all laughing. I said, "Aunt Minnie, remind me to never complain about my aches and pains when I come home!"

Sometimes circumstances in life seemed a bit hopeless. Mother would often say, "I'd cry if it would do any good!" Then she would look me right in the eye and laugh. I don't know how she did it, but I learned that sometimes we laugh to keep from crying.

Myrtice Nygaard Larson - my sister

The person in my life who has done the most outstanding things with her life has been my sister, Myrtice. She is absolutely the epitome of strength and class. She always knew since she was a child that she would some day be a teacher. She also had a boyfriend at six years of age, who later became her husband. She was able to combine her marriage with her professional life, and did a great job at both.

Myrtice taught at every grade level, first grade through seniors in college. She taught at Appalachian State Teachers College in Boone, N.C. and also at the University of North Texas in Denton. She was an outstanding leader in all the organizations to which she belonged, which means she was always an officer of some group.

She was president of many local and state organizations, as well as the first female in the American Lutheran Church Synod ever to serve a congregation as its president. She was entered into "Who's Who of Texas Education" and "Who's Who of American Education," as well as being entered into the "Notable Women of Texas". Myrtice was also Arlington (Texas) "Senior Citizen of the Year" because of her volunteer service. She became Administrative Supervisor in McKinney; then Consultant for Elementary Education in Arlington.

Myrtice's husband, Curtis Larson, became a school principal in Arlington, Texas, after teaching fifth and sixth grades for a number of years. Curtis died of cancer after 32 years of marriage, but they will always be remembered for their contribution to Texas education. In 1997, Arlington Independent School District Board of Education named a new school the "Academy at Myrtice and Curtis Larson Elementary School", in Arlington, Texas.

Myrtice served two one-year terms as President of Texas Retired Teachers Association. Through her leadership for increased membership for coordinated efforts of TRTA (Texas Retired Teachers Association) and TRS (Teachers Retirement System of Texas), and for persuasive lobbying with legislators, Texas retired teachers received the largest annuity increase ever legislated in Texas. She still has the pen which then Governor George W. Bush handed to her after he signed the bill. Three years earlier she had served as President of Texas Elementary Principals and Supervisors Association.

Myrtice was designated as the recipient of the E.L. Galyean Service Award in 2006. It is the highest education award in Texas, and was presented to her at the State Convention of the Texas Retired Teachers Association which met in Amarillo.

She has put so much hard work and a deep passion into everything she has done. Why wasn't I surprised when she was voted an officer of every organization that she joined? People who are willing to work like that are few and far between.

Myrtice and I were roommates in college at North Texas University. She was always fun to be with, but was a "no nonsense" date who demanded respect. Once a couple of guys drove up, and honked as they arrived. She kicked the screen door open and yelled, "We don't give curb service!" I thought it was funny, but she meant it, so we stood there until they walked up to the door.

Later in life, Myrtice took a millinery course and learned to make beautiful hats. The people at my church said they always wondered which of my many hats I would wear each Sunday. Many were the pill boxes made popular by Jackie Kennedy when Jack Kennedy was our president. I had silk, satin, ultra-suede, leather, and fur hats. I guess someone else thought they were pretty, too, as all were stolen one summer when I went home to take care of my mother during her last month of life. Not long after that, the hippies were the rage, with their flower-power and casual life-style. Dressing up with hats and gloves were out of fashion.

I believe Myrtice was always a little worried that I would be fired, because I lived on the edge, but there was never a problem. I would remind her that there was a teacher shortage in Texas. Anyway, the greatest compliment I would receive from teachers and students, was that they had never met a teacher like me! I taught 38 years and Myrtice taught for 40 years! Her retirement gift to me was a 10-day trip to Hong Kong with her. I told her I wanted to see if it was a two-way ticket, just in case she was thinking of dumping me over there!

I spend much of my time with my brother and sister. Noran is "laid back" and full of one-line quips. On the other hand, Myrtice has always been disciplined, but it is her determination that has propelled her to the heights of recognition in her profession. I call them "the jester" and "the general".

Olney Noran Nygaard–my twin

The very best friend I've ever had has been my twin brother, Noran. Unlike many siblings, we always got along well together. He is a lot like my mother and my dogs. He's patient, never judgmental, and doesn't advise or criticize me! I believe twins are attuned to each others thinking, so you know how the other person feels or thinks without having to probe. In other words, he knows when to talk, and knows when to walk!

Of course, being in the same grade, we ran around with the same friends, so we had much in common. We also had a $100.00 bet going for years that the other twin would marry first. We both loved being our own boss, and not having to give an account of our every move to anyone! Neither of us cared to date the same person every night, THAT'S CALLED MARRIAGE! We always figured that married life was way over-rated in the first place!

It turned out that I was married for three and one-half years and he was married for three and three-fourth years. I asked him later how he managed to be so patient and stay married for such a long time. We both had the determination that no one would ever tie us down again. What was unbelievable was that for over 20 years we lost contact with each other, yet we married about the same time, and divorced about the same time. We were almost 40 years old when we made the earth-shattering mistake.

When I got a divorce, my ex-husband gave me the record, "Born Free". He asked me to marry him again at the time of the divorce. I said, "I'll guaranDAMNtee you, that will never happen again!" I should have given him the Patsy Cline record, "I'm Crazy for Loving You". Instead, I took a few tranquilizers, and went on with my life.

Likewise, Noran's wife didn't want him to leave. She told him he would never find anyone like her. He replied, "I hope to hell you're right". In 1974, Noran attended a dance in Spokane, Washington with music by the country singer, Ernest Tubb and his band, the Texas Troubadors. During intermission, albums were being sold so he bought one and was instructed to take it to Ernest Tubb for an autograph. As he handed the album to Tubb, Noran said, "While you are writing, I will tell you a quick personal story. A couple of years ago, at my divorce party, I was talking to a neighbor and told him my attitude about the divorce was like the country singer, Ernest Tubb, when he sings the song with the line 'No regrets, no hard feelings, it's over!' The neighbor replied, 'There's another one by Roy Clark called 'Thank God and the Greyhound, You're Gone!'" Mr. Tubb seemed to enjoy Noran's story and his appreciation for Country Music.

We still like all the big band music of the 40's and 50's, but Noran also likes a lot of western music. He sings songs like, "All My Ex's Live in Texas"(even though she didn't and one was enough for him). When I play the accordion, my theme song is "Born to Lose". We dated many others, but if they started getting serious, we would (in his words) cut the trail!

We both had deep appreciation for country and western music, as well as for big band music. It is our firm conviction that without the humorous quips by Bob Hope and the music provided by great band leaders of that time, victory by the allies in World War ll may not have been accomplished. Some of the popular band leaders were:

Glen Miller, Tommy Dorsey, Harry James. and Benny Goodman, who also contributed entertainment for the military servicemen and women.

I believe that being single is the greatest feeling of freedom anyone can ever experience. There are few days that I forget to thank the Good Lord that I'm FREE—FREE AT LAST!

Noran still has a great sense of humor. On our last birthday, October 22, I told him that I would be mixing a margarita or two before we would go to lunch. I always give him a pair of Reebok shoes for his birthday; black ones for fall and winter, and at Christmas, I give him white ones for spring and summer. Well, he came up with a birthday card that was so fitting and funny that I still laugh every time I read it. I have always loved dogs–and here is a dog holding up a drink and making a toast. It says:

<u>Here's to You on Your Birthday!</u>

Here's to a perfect day and year!
Here's to a lifetime of good cheer!
Here's to fine wine, food, and song! (tail is wagging)
'N here's to workdays that aren't too long!
Here's to shoes that always fit (dog has lamp shade on his head)
'N here's to you   (dog is falling backwards)
You shilly sit! (On the inside of the card; the dog is balancing
a drink on his nose)

(As to aging, I agree with Maxine (the greeting card character) who says, "Take every birthday with a grain of salt. This works much better if the salt accompanies a margarita.")

(As I went through a box of pictures, I found this poem which I wrote 50 years ago, and decided it deserved being in this chapter with the most important characters of my life, because of all the love I poured out to someone special)

You say I cannot love you
Cause I haven't known you long?
Life is but a moment;
Love, a joyful song.

Each day I shall remember
The way you held me tight.
The way you kissed my tears away;
The way we said goodnight.

May someday I be near you;
May the joys of love be ours;
We'll laugh and play beneath the sun
And love beneath the stars.

Perhaps I should forget you;
But can I forget your smile?
You brought me happiness and love,
And made my life worthwhile.

(My only problem is —I have no earthly idea for whom I wrote this. I probably had cold feet and decided not to deliver it. I was about as afraid of marriage as I was of a rattlesnake! So –- for whomever this was intended, you were very special to me at that time!)

I always felt fortunate to have had so many good friends and nice romances. I do want it to be known, however, that I had a high regard for the institution of marriage. It's just that the thought of being "institutionalized" for the rest of my life didn't appeal to me!

My Most Unforgettable Sermon - "Fountain of Youth"

(As I rummaged through a box of my old memoirs, I came across my most unforgettable sermon, by Pastor William Blessing of Denver, Colorado. I have held on to this since January 1957. I will try to summerize it.)

FOUNTAIN OF YOUTH – FOR YOU

Jesus Christ was in his thirty-fourth year when He was raised from the dead. He has not aged since then. He will always be in his thirty-fourth year.

You were dead and buried with Him. You were baptized into Christ. The Bible says: "We are members of His body, of His flesh and of His bones." (Eph. 5:30) We received His body and His blood (Matt. 26:26-27, John 6:48-58) "Let this mind be in you, which was also in Christ Jesus." (Phil. 2:5) "We have the mind of Christ." (1 Cor. 2:16) "If the spirit of Him that raised up Jesus from the dead dwells in you, He that raised up Christ from the dead shall also quicken (give life to) your mortal bodies by His Spirit that dwelleth in you." (Rom. 8:11) Read it again. THINK - MEDITATE - BELIEVE.

We are the BODY - the flesh, blood, mind, soul and Spirit of Christ. Therefore, we should physically forever remain in our 34th year. CHRIST is the Eternal Fountain of Youth. CHRIST is our

YOUTH and HEALTH. Just believe and accept this truth. That's all there is to overcoming the world. That's all there is for you to do to become young and healthy again. Don't try to do it yourself. Let go and let God! His yoke is easy; His burden is light - and ye shall find REST, PEACE, CALMNESS, and VICTORY in your BODY, MIND, SOUL, and SPIRIT - and everything you do will prosper. Be still! Let God do the work through you.

The stress and strain, red tape and tension in the world will kill you unless you get the victory over the world - which is the CHRIST IN YOU. Don't be worried or hurried; take it easy. Ask and ye shall receive, seek and ye shall find, knock and it shall be opened unto you.

ALL THINGS ARE YOURS. Open up and receive everything that you want. More will come to you than you can receive. Work will be easy and a real pleasure.

Jesus said, "Verily, verily I say unto you, he that believeth in Me, the works that I do, shall he do also; and greater works than these shall he do! (John 14:12) Faith is the God substance, the creative element out of which all things are made. By using the element of faith we can overcome the world. We can control the world. We can do all things, have all things, and be anything that we wish to be. This is the secret truth and you have the knowledge and power by which you can stay young and can be healthy, wealthy and happy.

God is real and His power is great and it's high time that you realize that He can help you right here and now. TODAY! RIGHT NOW!

Pastor Blessing told of many people in biblical days who lived long lives - some lived over 900 years. But the story that I enjoyed most was about Abraham who was 100 years old and Sarah was 90 when Issac was born. Both had been old and decrepit, yet God restored them their youth. After that, Sarah became the most beautiful woman that the world has ever known. All the kings of the Middle East wanted her. Abraham was 140 years old when he married Keturah and he fathered six children by her and lived to be 175 years old. So, remember ladies and gentlemen, you're never too old. I think it would be fun to become beautiful, healthy, and young again - but I'm not looking for a 140 year old husband!

King Olav V (the 5th) - Norway

Speaking of kings, I did have an unforgettable meeting with King Olav V on October 10, 1982. My dad was so excited when he heard the King of Norway would be attending the Norse Lutheran Church where he had grown up, near Clifton. So I went out and bought a new dress to wear so Myrtice and I could take our dad to meet the King of Norway.

King Olav arrived at our Savior's Lutheran Church grounds, via helicopter as First Calvary Division Band and Color Guard from Fort Hood, Texas played "God's Word is Our Great Heritage". The people who were members of that church went inside, along with the King. The remaining crowd was seated outside in chairs under the shade trees. There were several loud speakers outside, so everyone could hear the church service.

After the church service, everyone gathered in the cemetery where King Olav laid a wreath of flowers on Cleng Peerson's grave. It was a celebration of the 200th anniversary of the birth of Cleng Peerson who earned the title, "The Father of Norwegian Immigration to America." Cleng Peerson was known to be a very kind and unselfish man who devoted his life to helping others. He died in 1865 at the age of 82.

We left the cemetery and went to Clifton for a tea party honoring King Olav V. It was in a room much too small for the size of the crowd, and was on the grounds where I had gone to Clifton Junior

College. We were packed in that building like a "can of Norwegian sardines".

I stepped back to let some people pass who were carrying refreshments. And you guessed it! I almost knocked the king down - and all I could say was, "Your Majesty, I can't believe this!" I started laughing - and King Olav also laughed.

His week's tour of Texas included an airport ceremony in Dallas, Texas. He was greeted by the Ambassador of Norway, City of Dallas dignitaries, and the Norwegian Society of Texas Representatives. He was presented with a bouquet of Texas yellow roses. In the afternoon he proceeded to the State Fair of Texas for a ribbon cutting ceremony, led by governor William Clements. He ended his stay in Texas by visiting Houston, the Norwegian Seaman Center, and a tour of the Houston Ship Channel.

I'm sure His Majesty's visit to the Lone Star State was a memorable one.

George McGee

Victoria (Vickie) Copeland
Fun! Fun! Fun! That's all
you think about!

Johnny Ghirardi

Jean Williams

Sue Thompson

Holly Westerberg

Delores (Patterson)
Cranfill (Best friends
for 66 years!)

Philo Harvey

Mary Johnson

great deals

Let's make a DEAL–
Send me the funniest joke you've ever heard,
and I'll send you my recipe for honey-glazed
baby-back barbeque ribs! Deal?

Norene Nygaard
2114 Rickel Park Drive #227
Hurst, Texas 76053

Please send self-addressed stamped envelope.

Lord, make me as good as my dogs think I am.

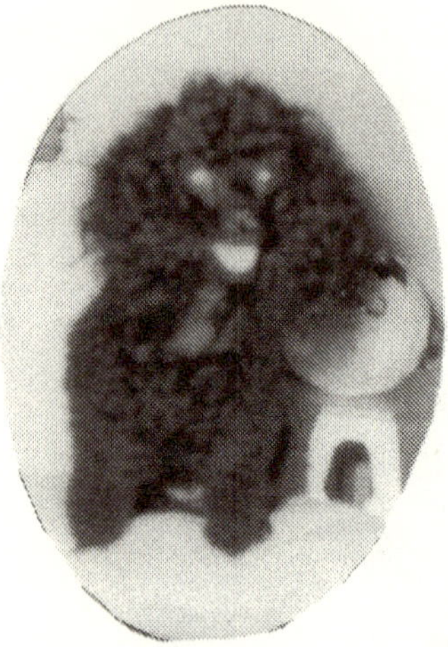

Jeanie II

Jeanie I

Missy

A passion—little dogs, and big Cadillacs.

Chapter 11

My Dogs, My Friends, My Opinions

When my little black poodle, Jeanie died, my heart was broken. She was 14 years old. That's 98 dog years! I am not good at hiding my emotions. When she died, some friends had a florist deliver some beautiful flowers to my room at school. When I saw them, tears started rolling down my cheeks, and the children wondered what had happened. I told them that my dog had died. One little girl said, "Why didn't you tell us?"

I said that I didn't want to bring my sadness to them, and they all came up to my desk and hugged and kissed me until my tears stopped. That is what I like about little children -- so sweet and loving.

About a year later, my friends encouraged me to get another dog. I also named her Jeanie, because no matter what name I gave to her, I kept calling her Jeanie. So she became Jeanie ll. She was also a black poodle, but was taller with longer legs. She had been mistreated by another family, so I wanted her, so she would never have to be ill-treated again. When Daddy saw her, he laughed and said, "Well, if it isn't Too Tall!" (referring to the Cowboy football player, Ed "Too Tall" Jones.) They became best friends.

I always thought, "When I have a dog, what else do I need?" After about 14 years, she too, died.

Will Rogers once said, "If there are no dogs in Heaven, then when I die, I want to go where they went." I grew up admiring the talents of Will Rogers. I loved his movies, and still remember in which field I was working when I heard about his death in a plane crash.

About a year after Jeanie ll died, Mary and Sue were at their beauty shop and heard a friend saying that she was going to have to move , and would not be allowed to take her pets with her. She had a dog that was part poodle, and wanted to find a good home for it. They told her they knew just the right person who would give her pet a lot of love and attention. When I saw Missy, it was love at first sight. We had many wonderful times together. She also died at about 14 years of age. You never get over the death of a loyal pet. I often thought, "God, make me as good as my dogs think I am."

When Missy died, my heart was broken. As I was watching Christian Television, I heard Rexella and Jack Van Impe talk about a video they had made called, "Animals in Heaven". It mentions theologians like Dr. Billy Graham, Dr. John Calvin, and others who have studied the Bible and gave the chapters and verses that convinced them that our animals would be waiting for us in Heaven. I like the way the video ends with the question "Are you sure you will be there to meet them?

If not, get right with the Lord today." The thought that our beloved pets will be resurrected with us gave me comfort.

When I came to North Texas to a town called Hurst, I immediately liked all the teachers. We had many wonderful parties together. On payday, I would sometimes write on the blackboard in the teachers lounge, "Happy hour today at 4:00 p.m. (at a specified restaurant that served margaritas.) Shortly after arriving, I started getting acquainted with my neighbors. I met one interesting lady, Mary Johnson, who also had a poodle, and we got acquainted as we walked our dogs, and watched them play together.

She introduced me to her long-time friend, Sue Thompson, who later moved into our apartment complex. The three of us shopped, had walks in the park, and even more often, we went out to eat. I don't know how Sue and I became such good friends, as our personalities are complete opposites. I think everyone is pretty and she doesn't agree at all. I see beauty even in an old wrinkled face. Perhaps through my imaginary mind, I wonder if I can see just a glimpse of God in someone's eyes or smiles.

Sue doesn't care for animals while they have often been my best friends. But she's so immaculate, she can put me to shame. She irons and cleans house all the time. I "wash and wear" and only dust when I start sneezing. She's honest, and her morals are above reproach, so we tolerate each other's idiosyncrasies.

My next door neighbor, Holly Westerberg, is truly a good friend, and I don't know what I'd do without her. She's often there when I'm struggling up the stairs with an overload of groceries, and she's always ready to help me when my computer plays tricks on me. She does little things like putting in a light bulb to save me from having to climb on a stool or chair. But most of all, she was there to help me when I was in so much pain that my legs quit working for a day or two. She reminds me of my mother, also a quiet person, who lifts my spirits and says a prayer for me when I need it most.

Andria Arlotta also has been a good friend and neighbor. When Andria or Holly would leave town, I would take care of their cats. I am known around here as the "animal lady" because of my love for animals. When we get in a habit of helping others, we can be assured that God will send someone to help us when we are in need.

Even though we sometimes take care of each other, we can still enjoy the good times together. Having good neighbors and friends is like living life on a full tank. Friends have a way of making it easier to focus on life and they encourage us when our spirits are low. It's the God in each of us that takes an ordinary thing in life, and makes an extraordinary thing out of it.

Vickie Copeland has been like a sister since the mid 70's. She has had some real challenges with her health, yet she bubbles with the joy and love she spreads around to everyone . There is no one who doesn't love her as she has a way of making everyone feel so wonderful and special. I believe her secret is to be happy, live for the moment, and not worry about the future.

Most of my childhood friends have already gone to be with the Lord, but I have two long time friends, Delores Patterson (Cranfill) and Fay Hastings (Pendleton). We have been friends for over 65 years and we still keep in touch with each other. What a good feeling to know someone still likes you after all these years. When we get together, we share many memories.

My other longtime friends are Annabelle (Ann) Priest and her daughter, India Ann (Punkin) Priest (Taylor). We lived together for eight years, so we will always have a special bond. Because of all the time we spent together, you have already read much about them.

Ann knew many wealthy friends. She was fun to be with and was always so proper in the way that she presented herself. Faith, a friend of hers from California, told me about a funny episode. She was relaxing in a hammock one afternoon and over-heard a multi-millionaire ask Ann to marry him. When she heard Ann refuse his proposal, she flipped off the hammock, and as she fell, broke her tail bone! She hadn't realized that there were many other wealthy men interested in Ann. She didn't have to marry the first one who came along.

Sometimes it was convenient for me to go out with some of her male friends. John was often referred to as the most eligible bachelor in Dallas. He owned a beautiful house that had been designed by Frank Lloyd Wright. It had a beautiful pool, and a small artistically landscaped creek ran through his property.

George McGee had been my buddy in California for several years. He decided to move back to Dallas, Texas. I saw him only a couple of times, and then I heard he had died.

Philo, another of Ann's wealthy friends from California, had three homes . He was the main one I went with after I was divorced. The last time I saw him, he told me that his doctor said that his heart was failing.

He died a short time after our visit. I never dated anyone after he died.

As the saying goes, you know you are getting old when you have to look around to find a senior citizen your age. I also found out that at a certain age, if you don't wake up aching in every joint, you are probably already dead.

A Few Opinions to Many Problems

I see so many problems in America that makes me sad. How did the mentality of so many people allow drugs to get into our country? I wish the energy used in the constant bickering between the Republicans and the Democrats be used to figure out how to keep drugs from coming here and ruining the lives of so many Americans. Of course, people are supposed to use a little restraint, and learn to say "NO", but they seem to go blindly into something they know nothing about, then become addicted to something, which adds to many other problems.

The second largest problem in America in my opinion, is the misuse of credit cards. Too many people use credit cards unwisely. They give up everything for tomorrow to gain a little pleasure today. People are tempted and encouraged to use a pocket full of cards. When they have reached the limit, another card company comes along to HELP them! The young folks getting out of college are up to their necks in debt before they even start their first job. How exciting can that be? Where is the incentive to start earning and saving money? Yes, I know college costs a lot more now – however, jobs pay more, too. When I couldn't afford all the expenses, I found a job, either on or near the campus. I taught school all day and worked for a doctor after school to save enough money to go to college during the summer.

Teachers didn't get paid adequately for their time and effort, so I sold vitamins and cosmetics. I also started a dancing career to make a few extra dollars.

Owing money is much like slavery—someone else controls you. Even the Bible warns us not to get in debt. I cut up all but one credit card, which was to be used only in an emergency. No more was ever put on the card except what could be paid for at the end of the month.

Now, if I don't have cash to buy something, I don't buy it. That goes for everything from clothing to four Cadillacs which I bought with cash. It's a good feeling to feel FREE. I don't own a house, but I have a nice apartment which gives me access to a pool, and if anything goes wrong, the office staff promptly takes care of it. I would be a wreck if I thought I owed a penny for a place to live. If people want to complicate their lives by buying a house that never gets paid for, it is their own business. It's just not my "cup of tea" to be in debt.

America needs more parents who will instill values into the lives of their children. The mind is indeed a terrible thing to waste. Children need to be taught that it's fun to make their own money. The children also need to know there may be times when they may have to do things they don't want to do. But that will build their character. Teach them study skills, so that they can successfully strive toward their goals.

Most parents do a pretty good job. But you know, I know, and God knows, there are many children who are practically raising themselves. Many have been rejected and they need help! With a good moral and educational background, America can stay strong. Only then, will we see less stealing, killing, and fraud in the world. In other words, everyone needs to GET A JOB, be more independent and quit taking advantage of others! We live in the greatest country in the world. We need to take advantage of the opportunities, and make better lives for ourselves. Live the American Dream! I'd rather try to do something great and fail, than to do nothing and succeed.

I don't understand the appeal for all the violence and sex that is portrayed on TV and in all the movies. Is it any wonder that children are having problems?

I still remember the shock that people had in 1943 when Clark Gable said, "Frankly, my dear, I don't give a damn!" in the famous movie, "Gone With the Wind". If those people could hear and see the current movies, there would probably be more heart attacks. I am fairly certain that my story won't be made into a movie and I would like to challenge any actress who can pretend to do all the things I have done in my lifetime.

Having said that, I choose to get away from the bad and ugly, and for once, send out some good news. I am overwhelmed by the goodness in America.

I have seen people who would give the shirts off their backs to help others. When there's a catastrophe, people in our great country always come together to help the less fortunate.

The heroes are the ordinary people who do extraordinary things to help better the lives of others. You seldom get a chance to read in the news about these people, because the media is hell-bent on writing about all the violence and negativity in the world. There are also many religious groups who do an unbelievable amount of charity work that often goes unrecognized. Wouldn't it be refreshing for someone to come up with a newspaper which tells only about good things going on in the world?

I also have a high admiration for the rich and famous like Elizabeth Taylor and Oprah Winfrey. They have used their own money and talents for raising money to help people less fortunate. Of course, there are millions who do that, but these happen to be among my favorites whom I have followed through the years. Who can't admire someone like Liz Taylor, who had the guts to start getting help for Aids victims before the rest of the people would even talk about the horrible disease that was taking the lives of so many around the world. Oprah sees the need for education and through her encouragement in reading books, she now has a huge group of people in her book club. And now, of course, she has opened her own 40 million dollar school in which she intends to stay involved and follow through on their progress. Wow! And she started at the bottom like a lot of us. More recently, I've added Dr. Phil to that group of favorites who constantly help others to achieve better lives.

I have a friend, Dorothy Hopps, whom I admire so much because she has devoted her entire life to the Salvation Army. As a small child, she often accompanied her mother who had also dedicated her life to the Salvation Army. She played in the young people's band and took Bible courses for six years. When she graduated from high school, she went to the Salvation Army training college in Chicago and was commissioned as a lieutenant a year later. After some years she became a captain - then major. This year will be her 66th year as an officer. Dorothy is still very active in the Salvation Army. I especially enjoyed listening to her experiences that she shared during the Christmas holidays when they ministered at different Veterans Hospitals.

She played in the Salvation Army band as the group visited the various Veterans Hospitals. I was shocked to hear that at one place, they were not allowed to sing songs about Jesus, but could sing about Santa or holiday songs. What is happening to our country? God made this country great, and if we push Him out, our country will become weak. Believe me! We must stay strong.

Among others who have my admiration is Paul and Jan Crouch, who are the founders of Trinity Broadcasting Network (TBN), a Christian television station that reaches people all over the world. I have watched them since they began to fulfill their dream about 33 years ago. There are many ministers on that station who have dedicated their lives to saving souls for the Lord. And it doesn't stop there. When there is a hurricane or any kind of crisis, people like Pat Robertson and his son Gordon, of Christian Broadcasting Network

(CBN and the 700 Club) fame, greatly support Franklin Graham's (Billy Graham's son) "Operation Blessing". This ministry is often the first to arrive on the scene to feed and care for the unfortunate victims. I have heard people make remarks like, "If it were not for the Christians, I don't know what would have happened to us."

The Red Cross and Salvation Army are so well organized and with everyone's contributions, have helped millions of people. I listen to many others on television who really lift my spirits. I can see why God decided to have them spread the word for Him.

Most of the time, if I am relaxing, resting, or reminiscing, I am also giggling. My favorite pastime is reading or listening to jokes. We need more fun shows on television like "Everyone Loves Raymond". I have seen all the episodes so many times, I now know all the lines. But they will always be funny to me because their timing was the best I have heard or seen since the "I Love Lucy" and the "Carol Burnett" shows.

I hope that some day, some way, this country will wake up and realize that our future depends on education of the children, and that school teachers should be paid much more. Shouldn't teachers, with the same number of years in college get paid as much as doctors, lawyers, and other professional people? After all, they were trained by teachers! Athletes can be paid millions of dollars for playing a sport that they love, while teachers with all their training and required schooling should get only a small salary for all they do at school and the papers they have to take home to grade? It doesn't make sense! I am not against sports. I spent half my career teaching physical education to the future generation, but my salary over 38 years ranged from $200.00 to $2,000.00 a month, with most of the years being an average of about a $1,000.00 a month.

I always worked at least two jobs to get by, only I called one of them my hobby. I picked a hobby that would pay me instead of my having to pay for the pleasure of doing something in my spare time. Most of the time was spent teaching dancing, doing dance exhibitions, doing secretarial work for doctors, dance or modeling studios. I also did cosmetic parties at homes. Don't forget that after teaching school all day, teachers have a choice of staying after school and grading papers or bringing them home every day.

If something isn't done, there will only be a few teachers left. I have seen many teachers quit each year, especially the men after they were married and started a family. We lost many excellent teachers.

Since I retired, I have done networking for the last 20 years. I loved teaching but I am just pointing out that if we are going to have teachers for the future generations, someone needs to help them receive a decent salary, comparable to others who also have a college education.

I don't care how much a person loves to teach, no one ever said it would be easy. Sometimes the frustrations, yet feelings of responsibilities would overwhelm us. When I needed to relax my emotions, I would step into my closet for a minute. The closet was small, just a few shelves for storing my personal supplies and bulletin board charts, along with a hook to hang my coat. But that little closet helped me through many days. I had charts and pictures on the walls. One was a 8x12 picture of a donkey with the caption, "You can lead a horse to water, but you can't make him drink." Another said, "He who has lost faith in God has little to live for, and even less to die for".

But my favorite chart was written by a lady who was very knowledgeable. I don't know if she was a teacher or a psychiatrist. If teacher friends looked tired and disgusted, I knew they were having a "psychological moment".

I would ask them to step into my closet, and they came out smiling every time.

I still have the sign, though it has turned yellow with age. It reads,

"THE DAILY EFFORT TO TEACH IS AN EXPERIENCE
WHICH WOULD DRIVE MOST PEOPLE TO THE
VERGE OF A NERVOUS BREAKDOWN... WHICH
IS WHERE MOST CONSCIENTIOUS TEACHERS
SEEM TO BE MOST OF THE TIME."
--- Allison Davis

Noran and Norene-80 years old.

Won't it be fun dancing in Heaven?
No pain, no sorrow,—no riff-raff!

(found recently in an old Bible)
Thank you, God, for letting me
have such an enjoyable life. I
know I wasn't perfect, but you
sure covered for me a bunch of
times! Thanks! Amen. Norene.

Chapter 12

On Being a Christian - And Using Our God-Given Talents

I was brought up in the Lutheran Church, so needless to say, I had a good religious foundation. My goal each year was to receive the Perfect Attendance Sunday School Certificate. I spent two weeks of every summer in Bible School. I was in the choir, so I knew most of the songs in the hymnal. There is a saying, "He who sings hymns, prays twice." The beautiful words are caught up in the mind and in the heart of the person who sings. I studied two years of Bible when I attended Clifton Junior College. (I KNOW, YOU'RE WONDERING WHY MORE OF THIS DIDN'T RUB OFF ON ME!)

Many of us had the same training, and several friends became ministers. I figured if anyone from my group of friends became a minister, it would be my cousin, Truman Pederson. While we were in college at North Texas University, he drove over 100 miles to teach Sunday School in his home church. However, God didn't call him, or if He did, He didn't yell loud enough! Truman became a teacher. His first son, Joe Ed, did become a minister, and also served many years over-seas as a chaplain in the U.S. Army.

I liked going to church, but thank God, I didn't get a calling to preach. There were no women ministers in our church in those days. Speaking in front of a crowd was not my talent. I would freeze in front of an audience, and then I'd go into laughing hysterics. I've done that twice in college on test days. I think in the back of my mind I worried that I would make a grammatical error, or perhaps end a sentence with a preposition. So I would never have been hired—unless God knew someone so depressed, that they needed a good laugh!

I felt fortunate to get a teaching job. My methods of teaching were not always the same as the "fuddy-duddy" rules we learned in our Education classes in college. (I often wondered in which century the book had been written.) I believed learning could be more fun, so I did it my way! But I got every job I ever applied for, and was never fired!

I did believe in starting each day with a prayer, as we had done when I went to school. We often sang the national anthem or another patriotic song. I hope that prayer will again be allowed in all the classrooms. I once heard a minister say that when God was thrown out of the schools, was when the devil walked in. A rather startling statement; however, we didn't see guns, drugs or gangs in our schools until prayer was removed and morals and the love of God was excluded from our daily lives.

I wrote my "cut and dried" opinions of keeping prayer in schools while I was in Dallas, and sent it to The Dallas Morning News. To my surprise, it was published in the paper. I received a nice letter from Dr. Frank Williams, from the Dallas School Administration Building, who agreed with my opinion that prayer should be kept in the schools. Unfortunately, our efforts were to no avail.

I remember a cartoon that appeared in the Texas Outlook (a teachers magazine). It had some boys huddled together on the ground. The teacher was asking, "What's going on?" They said they were shooting craps.

The teacher said, "That's ok then, I was afraid you were praying!"

It breaks my heart to see some children grow up with very little moral values as well as a Christian upbringing at home, and teachers not being able to teach moral values.

Knowing that God gives you unlimited talents and the capacity to do anything you want to, we should use our talents to help others. REMEMBER, THAT WHAT YOU DO FOR YOURSELF IN LIFE DIES WITH YOU, BUT WHAT YOU DO FOR OTHERS REMAINS UNFORGETTABLE. I had friends who wanted to become better dancers, but instead of charging for lessons, I'd make a "deal" with them. I exchanged dance lessons for bowling lessons, golf lessons, and water skiing lessons.

When I learned to water ski, my friend showed me exactly how to come out of the water, how much to bend my knees, and to keep the correct posture. He and his friend got into the boat and away we went! What excitement! I lived for the rush! I remember thinking, "Look, Jesus–I'm on top of the water right beside you!"

My friend later told me that it was the first time he had seen a beginner ski all over the lake without falling. So I complimented him on his excellent teaching skills, while he complimented me on having strong legs. We both knew it was that extra power we get from God that made it such a successful experience! With God, you are able to do more than you can ask for or imagine! I could do nothing in my own strength. I didn't spend a lifetime going to church and not know where I obtained my ability and power to be able to do the things I needed to do.

I had another friend, Hank Schroder, who loved to dance. We have been friends for over 50 years. He managed a fast food chicken franchise in Dallas. When I wanted to sit at home and watch TV, I sometimes ordered some chicken to be delivered. If he were there, he would write "no charge" on the bill. In return, we often went dancing, and I would teach him and his Sunday School group some dance steps at a small country club where they were members. The men formed a line on one side and the women on the other side. We would have them walk through the new steps. Then Hank and I would demonstrate the lead and the follow-through, and they were ready to be put together to do a couple of steps at a time to the music!

Now, back to my being a Christian; the hardest part about being a Christian is for the "so-called Christian" to pick me to pieces on everything I say or do. I know that I'm a sinner, but so is everyone else. So why do I have to feel that people are hell-bent on beating me over the head with their Bibles?

I sometimes heard remarks like, "If you are a Christian, how do you explain dancing and going to "honky-tonks"?

I would usually turn it into a joke or riddle, by saying something like, "That's where the music is; wouldn't I look silly dancing without music? Besides, someone wrote a nice song about God loving honky-tonk angels."

I always knew that my dancing was a gift from God. Of course, I cared what people said, and I was sensitive to ways they wanted to twist it to hurt me. When I went to a dance studio and saw how quickly I learned all the steps, I realized, that without God's help, a person couldn't normally absorb 140 dance steps in the short time I learned them. As I started to do an exhibition, a wonderful feeling of joy and confidence would come over me, and I knew it was the power of God that made me feel exhilarated and full of animation. IT WAS ALMOST AS THOUGH I WERE DANCING WITH GOD!

Another question I often got; "Is a Christian supposed to be sipping wine?"

I would answer, "When Jesus was at a wedding, and they were running out of wine, what did He do?" (Well, anyone who has read the Bible knows He turned some water into wine, so that everyone could dance, party, and have a good time.) Then I would add, to shock them a little, "My friend, Jesus, really knew how to throw a party!"

I asked, "Why do you think the people drank so much wine during the Biblical days?"

My friend answered, " The water wasn't very good in those days. So wine was better to drink than water."

To which I answered, "It still is!" Sometimes, I had to turn remarks into jokes or riddles to get my point across. All I can say is that I am glad that I will only have God to judge me. I am a long way from perfect, but I am fortunate to have a friend like Jesus who died for all my stupid, crazy, sins.

I was even told when I taught Sunday School that it sounded like I was serving both God and the devil. I said, "On the contrary, God has taken a heavy yoke off my neck, because I know the truth, and the truth has made me free!" SEEK FIRST THE KINGDOM OF GOD AND THE REST SHALL BE GIVEN UNTO YOU.

I know that it was by the grace of God, I made it through some difficult times. He never left me, and He never will. He looked beyond my faults and saw my needs. We cannot even imagine what God has prepared for all those who love Him.

I am nothing more than a sinner who has accepted God's grace! Even though God took the one (Brady) who was so special to me, He filled my life with so many other people and things.

I know that if God hadn't been on my side, I wouldn't have been able to have had such a full life. Being under the horoscope sign of Libra, I have tried to keep my life balanced so the scales show that I have balanced my professional life with my recreational and religious life. I could not have felt well-rounded had any part of it been excluded.

I DON'T KNOW WHAT OTHERS THINK, AND MOST OF THE TIME I DON'T CARE, but I have always felt that Jesus has a sense of humor, and we have had many laughs together. Lord, it's been a great ride!

Mother had a couple of favorite sayings, "If you can't say anything good, don't say anything at all" and "Sometimes, it's best not to say anything."

Since then, I try to remember that silence is often the best answer.

I like the feeling of freedom, and being able to open my mind to new ideas, avenues, and adventures - then advancing to the next level of activity.

I believe that God has great plans for everyone who will seek the truth. Everyone should put God first in their life and do the best that can be done.

In return, many blessings will befall that person.

This book is not "all about me". It includes many references about how God's presence was felt during trials of my life. It is also about people who have been an influence on my life.

I don't have a mansion, a fancy car, or a lot of money. What I have is not measurable. I have lots of memories and the peace and strength of God to sustain me every day.

My advise to the weary is to live an honest and honorable life, so in the "golden years" there may be a bountiful supply of happy, or funny, memories. Every day of your life is a special occasion.

One of my favorite quotations is, "Live life to the fullest; make every day a holiday and every meal a banquet." When we maintain a positive attitude, we can express a happier attitude with others who need a lift.

I am getting older now, and the old rocking chair embraces me for a great part of each day, but I can concentrate, meditate, imitate, exaggerate and even speculate. At times I can even agitate and aggravate.

No matter how positive you try to be, there will be many times in life when you might feel like a loser. But just remember, "IF YOU DON'T KNOW THE PAIN OF LOSING, HOW CAN YOU KNOW THE JOY OF WINNING?"

My entire life could probably be summarized in one verse from the Bible.

"To everything there is a season, a time for every purpose under heaven: a time to weep, a time to laugh, a time to mourn, and a time to dance.

~~~ Ecclesiastes 3:1, 4

Help Me, Dear Lord

Help me to know Thy ways, dear Lord;
Help me to do Thy will.
Give me the strength to face turmoil,
And let my heart be still.

Show me how to understand
Disappointments along the way.
Teach me to follow the laws of the land
And how to live each day.

Make me a better person
Than I've ever been before;
Give me the inner light that glows
And opens wide my door.

Inspire me, Lord, to greater heights;
May the joys of work I find.
Aid me in doing a better job
In helping all mankind.

And now, for all the wrong I've done -
Forgiveness, I implore;
Teach me patience, love, and smiles,
That I may offer more.

Help everyone to know Thy love;
The grace that it imparts,
The strength and comfort it bestows
To all believing hearts.

Watch o'er my body and soul, dear Lord
So when this life on earth is done,
Joys will be mine forever,
And the battle of life will be won.

I am not a public speaker, nor a writer, but I hope that in some way my book will inspire someone to become closer to God. Even though we are not as great as we would like to be, God takes us just as we are, and showers us with many blessings. And don't forget, the best is yet to come!

DALLAS INDEPENDENT SCHOOL DISTRICT
DALLAS, TEXAS
————
SCHOOL ADMINISTRATION BUILDING
3700 ROSS AVENUE
TELEPHONE VICTOR 1621

December 19, 1952

Dear Miss Nygaard,

This morning as I was eating my breakfast, I heard the
very lovely poem that you wrote read over the radio.
I don't believe that I have ever heard the inner thoughts
of a teacher so revealed in words. I know, as do all
teachers, exactly what you meant, and it was so nice to
have this message given out to people.

May you have a very Merry Christmas and a Happy New Year.

Sincerely,

R H McKay

Miss Norene Nygaard
417 South Oak Cliff Boulevard
Dallas, Texas

May 25, 1960

Dear Noren,

May I give you my very personal thanks for the fine work you have done in our Church School during the past few years. You have served your parish well, and have made a good contribution to the growing lives of many children. I want you to know how much this has been appreciated. My best wishes to you in any future work you do in the Church.

Sincerely,

Miller Cragon

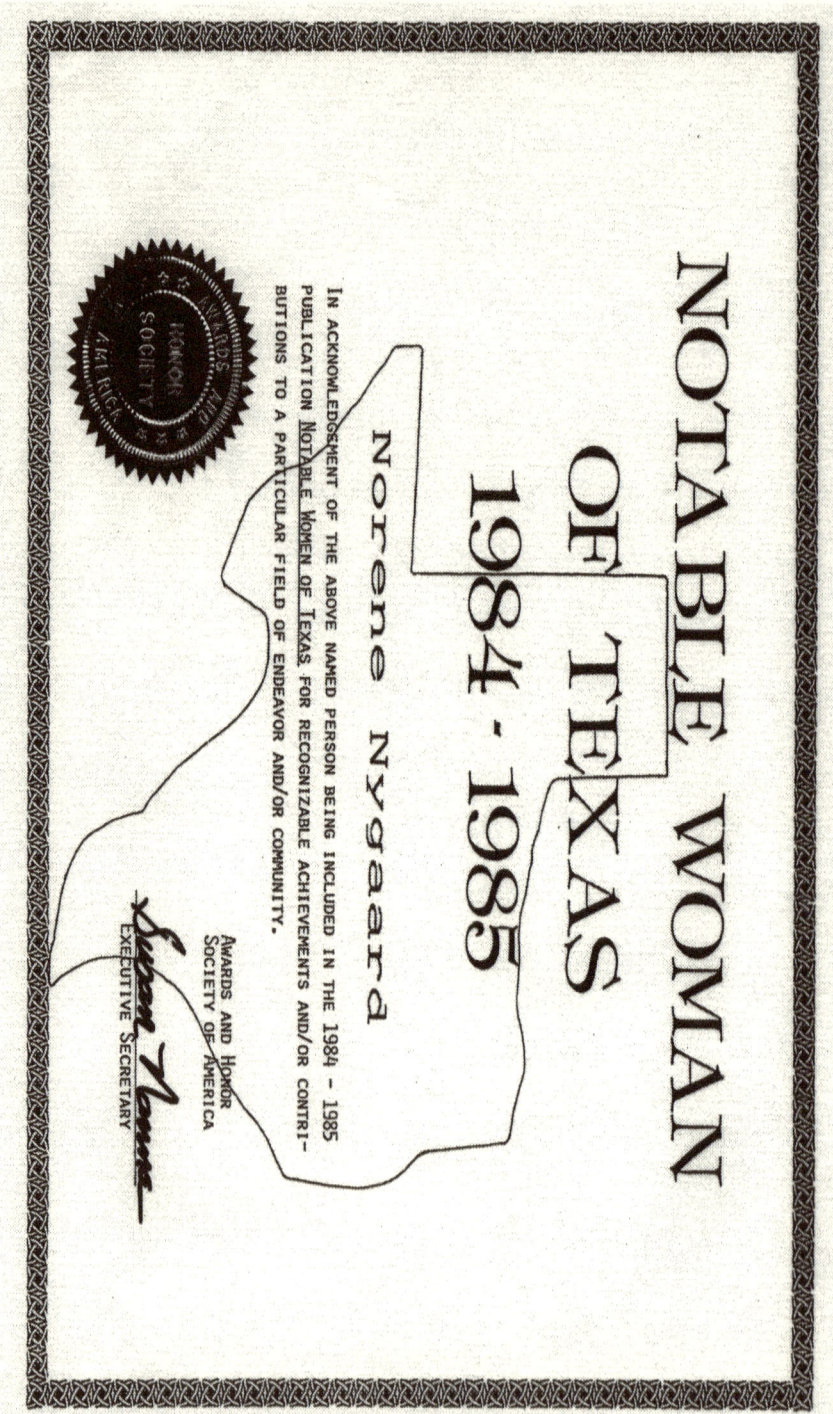

NOTABLE WOMAN OF TEXAS
1984 - 1985

Norene Nygaard

IN ACKNOWLEDGEMENT OF THE ABOVE NAMED PERSON BEING INCLUDED IN THE 1984 - 1985 PUBLICATION Notable Women of Texas, FOR RECOGNIZABLE ACHIEVEMENTS AND/OR CONTRIBUTIONS TO A PARTICULAR FIELD OF ENDEAVOR AND/OR COMMUNITY.

AWARDS AND HONOR
SOCIETY OF AMERICA

EXECUTIVE SECRETARY

When I retired in 1984, I was presented with a photo album from the Midway Park School. Each teacher presented a page. Many mentioned the 13 years we shared as friends at school. Most were about fun and silly pictures we took at some of our parties, especially when I danced at our favorite Mexican restaurant at the end of each year. But the following letter was one of my favorite pages written by Mr. Brown, who was the custodian of our school.

To say, "Beauty is in the eyes of the beholder", is to say anyone who look upon you and don't see beauty, is completely sightless.

For one to have lived as you have, accomplished what you have, traveled as you have traveled, and still be the caring, considerate, loving, sincere, God-fearing person that you are, is truly a thing of beauty. It has been a great pleasure working with you. I feel that in some way, youhave touched each and everyone that has come in contact with you.

Being the father of five (5) girls, I can only hope that (1) one grows up to be the person that you are.

As you launch your ship upon one of life's many oceans; with God as your navigator, I can only say,.............HAPPY SAILING.

Luv Ya,

Oscar C Brown Jr.

HURST-EULESS-BEDFORD

INDEPENDENT SCHOOL DISTRICT

In appreciation
for your generous contribution
to the children of this district
by

YOUR SERVICE OF THIRTEEN YEARS IN THE

HURST-EULESS-BEDFORD INDEPENDENT SCHOOL DISTRICT

NORENE NYGAARD

MAY 18, 1984
date

Neil W. Adams
President, Board of Trustees

Ernest E. Watson
Superintendent of Schools

212

www.ingramcontent.com/pod-product-compliance
Lightning Source LLC
Chambersburg PA
CBHW031320290526
45784CB00014B/288